Raspberry Pi Python Projects
Python3 and Tkinter/Ttk
Digital Clock, Temperature, Tactile Button Counter, Ultra Sonic Sensor,
Servo Control, Stepper Motor, DC Motor, Infrared Detector, Robot Follow Line, Color Sensor,
Joy Stick Thumb Control, Two Wheel Balance Bot

First Edition

Herb Norbom

Author of:
Python3.3.4 Tkinter/Ttk Widgets and Sqlite3
Raspberry Pi GPS using Python For Windows and Debian-Linux
Raspberry Pi Camera Controls For Windows and Debian-Linux using Python 3.2
Raspberry Pi Camera Controls For Windows and Debian-Linux using Python 2.7
Raspberry Pi Robot with Camera and Sound
Raspberry Pi Robot with Camera and Sound using Python 3.2.3
Robot Wireless Control Made Simple with Python and C
Python Version 2.6 Introduction using IDLE
Python Version 2.7 Introduction using IDLE
Python Version 3.2 Introduction using IDLE and PythonWin
Bootloader Source Code for ATMega168 using STK500 For Microsoft Windows
Bootloader Source Code for ATMega168 using STK500 For Debian-Linux
Bootloader Source Code for ATMega328P using STK500 For Microsoft Windows
Bootloader Source Code for ATMega328P using STK500 For Debian-Linux
Books Available on Amazon and CreateSpace

Table of Contents

FOREWARD...2
CAUTION..3
Simple Test...3
Summary of Supplies Purchased...3
Tactile Button/Switch...5
Digital Clock..9
Temperature..11
Temperature with LED..13
Temperature PWM control Fan...17
Converting Integer to Hex and Binary...24
Stop Python Program..26
Ultra Sonic Sensor..28
Analog Thumb Joy Stick...31
Servo Control..36
Stepper Motor Control...40
Color Sensor...48
DC Motors Robot..56
Robot Follow Black Tape..62
DC Motors Infrared Detectors...72
Balance Bot..80
   MPU6050CALIBRATION...81
   Balance Bot..88
Thank You...95

FOREWARD

Congratulations on selecting Python and the Raspberry Pi, you have made great choices. Python is a dynamic and relatively easy to use interpretive programming language. Python is available for most computer operating systems, and your Python programs can be relatively easily ported between the various operating systems. Python has a very good standard GUI in Tkinter/Ttk.

The Raspberry Pi is an amazing device. The Pi 3 has many features including built in WiFi and Bluetooth.

This book includes the printed source code and wiring diagrams for various projects. The electronic or digitized source code is available to download for an additional fee and for a limited time. The download includes the programs printed in this book, color PDF circuits and variations of some programs with extra features. Some programs are without Tkinter. Visit the web site www.rymax.biz for information. A limited time Discount is available. The Discount code is listed later in this book.

The projects are intended as learning tools, use them as starters for your projects.

All the code has been developed and tested on a Raspberry Pi 3.

GPIO Board version: 10
GPIO version: 0.6.3
GPIO RPI_Revision: 3
Python version: 3.4.2

Tkinter version: 8.6
OS version: Raspbian GNU/Linux 8 (jessie)
All the projects have been developed running from the command line using "python3 program.py".

Geany 1.24.1, was used as the program editor or IDE, it is included with this version of Raspbian. Note, you may need to set the build command as python3"%f". I have found that you will not need to run any of the programs using "sudo". If you find programs do not work without sudo check your versions. Tkinter does not work as installed if you run a program using sudo. I use "tab" vs space for indenting. You will notice in the printed source code that some lines are continued on multiple lines. Generally Python code can be split to a separate line on a ",". A line continuation character of "\" can also be used.

CAUTION

Handle your Raspberry and components with caution, static electricity is NOT YOUR FRIEND. While we have tried to ensure accuracy with all information please check everything and make sure it makes sense to you. As voltages increase the chances of damaging your Raspberry and/or components increases. **We will not be responsible for any damages**, you must ensure that all instructions work correctly for you.

Your Raspberry needs to do proper shutdowns, do not just power off.

Simple Test

Run the following program from the command line as python3 simpleTest.py

#quick and simple test to ensure python3 and tkinter are working

```
from tkinter import *
from tkinter.ttk import *


if __name__=="__main__":
    root = Tk()
    root.title("Simple Python3 and Tkinter Test")
    root.geometry("400x130x+1+10) # width, height, x location, y location
    print("Hello from Python3")
    root.mainloop()
```

Summary of Supplies Purchased

This is a list of possible suppliers. To lower shipping cost I have tried to source from as few vendors as possible. I am not affiliated with any of the suppliers. You will of course need a Raspberry. I highly recommend that you have a large SD. Parts can be purchased from www.adafruit.com A good reason to use Adafruit is for their product libraries. The Temperature Sensor, Analog to Digital converter, Servo Driver and Color Sensor require a FREE download of their libraries. Another good source is http://www.sparkfun.com/, they also have many good references.

Another good source is Electronix Express http://www.elexp.com/ in particular for resistors and capacitors. Consider some of the kits they offer.
In some of my examples I have used similar parts from different sources. The Stepper Motor is an

example of this. I purchased mine from MiniInTheBox, and the example has different gearing than the one shown in the table below from Adafruit.

If you do not have a Raspberry Pi you may want to consider a kit such as Adfruit Pi3 Starter Pack. ID3058. You will need a SD with greater capacity, I suggest a minimum of 16GB. Also install the Raspbian Jessie OS. I am not going to cover how to install it. A good starting point is https://www.raspberrypi.org/downloads/. Prices and availability subject to change.

Part Description	Vendor	Product ID	Project Used On	Price
Raspberry Pi 3	Adafruit	ID: 3055	ALL	$39.95
Raspberry Pi Case (Optional)				
5V 2.4A Switching Power Supply	Adafruit	ID: 1995	ALL	$7.50
SD Card suggest minimum 16Gb			ALL	
Assembled Pi Cobbler Plus – Breakout Cable	Adafruit	ID: 2029	MANY	$6.95
Full size breadboard (recommended but half size will work with most of the projects).	Adafruit	ID: 239	MANY	$5.95
Premium Male/Male Jumper Wires – 20 x6"	Adafruit	ID: 1957	MANY	$1.95
Premium Female/Female Jumper Wires 20x6	Adafruit	ID: 1950	MANY	$1.95
Premium Female/Male Jumper Wires 20x6	Adafruit	ID:1954	MANY	$1.95
MCP9808 High Accuracy i2c Temperature Sensor Breakout Board requires soldering	Adafruit	ID: 1782	3	$4.95
Tactile Button switch (6mm) x 20 pack	Adafruit	ID: 367	1	$2.50
Ultra Sonic Sensor HC-SR04 available on Amazon, Ebay, Sparkfun	Sparkfun	SEN-13959	4	$3.95
Resistor Kit prices vary by kit	Electronix Express			
Capacitor Kit prices vary by kit	Electronix Express			
Individual Resistors 470 OHM (25pack)	Adafruit	ID:2781	4, 7, 8, 9, 10, 11	$0.75
Individual Resistors 330 OHM (20pack)	Sparkfun	COM-11507	4	$0.95
ADS1015 12-Bit ADC-4 Channel with Programmable Gain Amplifier (requires soldering)	Adafruit	ID: 1083	5,10	$9.95
Analog Thumb Joy Stick, two potentiometers FIND BEST PRICE many vendors	MiniInThe Box		5	$1.99
Adafruit 16-Channel 12-bit PWM/ServoDriver -i2c interface PCA9685 (requires soldering)	Adafruit	ID:815	6	$14.95

Part Description	Vendor	Product ID	Project Used On	Price
Tower Pro SG92 Micro Servo	Adafruit	ID:169	6	$5.95
Small Reduction Stepper Motor 5VDC	Adafruit	ID:858	7	$4.95
Hobby Gearmotor -200 RPM(Pair) I like these as leads are solder already(But ROB-13258 work)	Sparkfun	ROB: 13302	MANY	$3.95
Wheels -65mm(Rubber Tire, Pair)	Sparkfun	ROB:13259	MANY	$2.95
H-Bridge Motor Driver	Sparkfun	COM:00315	MANY	2.35
RGB Color Sensor White LED TCS34725 (requires soldering)	Adafruit	ID: 1334	8, 9	7.95
SparkFun RedBot Sensor – Line Follower **NEED 2** of these for project	Sparkfun	SEN-11769	10	2.95
MPU6050 6 Axis Gyro Accelerometer Module (may require soldering)	MiniInThe Box.com		11	3.99
Battery Pack for Raspberry (Optional) Many sources check specs to ensure correct voltage and mAh. I like one that has on/off switch.	Adafruit Sparkfun others			

Project	Code
Tactile Button/Switch	1
Digital Clock	2
Temperature	3
Ultra Sonic Sensor	4
Analog Thumb Joy Stick	5
Servo Control	6
Stepper Control	7
Color Sensor	8
DC Motor for robot	9
DC Motor Infrared Detector	10
Balance Bot	11

Tactile Button/Switch

This program counts the number of times you press the Tactile Button. The count is displayed on the tkinter window. The program uses threading so that exit control can easily be provided. Threading use will be much more relevant as the other programs are developed.

#for python: 3.4.2 on Raspberry Pi   ButtonPressTkinter.py

```python
# number of times button pressed displayed in window
import time
from time import sleep
from tkinter import *
from tkinter.ttk import *
import threading
from threading import Thread
import RPi.GPIO as GPIO
GPIO.setmode(GPIO.BCM)
GPIO.setup(18, GPIO.IN, pull_up_down = GPIO.PUD_UP)


class SELF:
        pass                    # set up, define later as needed
SELF.myCounter = 0      # counter for number of times button pressed

def Setup():
        SELF.bF=LabelFrame(root,text="Button Control",width=90,height=90)
        SELF.bF.grid(column=0,columnspan=4,row=0)
        Button(SELF.bF, text='EXIT', command=stopALL).grid(column=0,row=0)
        Label(SELF.bF,text= "Button Press Count",
                        width=20).grid(column=0,row=1)
        Label(SELF.bF,text= SELF.myCounter).grid(column=2,row=1)

def stopALL():
        GPIO.setup(18, GPIO.OUT)
        GPIO.cleanup()
        sleep(.2)
        root.destroy()

def displayUPDATING():
        while True: #running via thread so can have control to start it
            try:
                    myInputState = GPIO.input(18)
                    if (myInputState ==0):    # False or Zero,
                        SELF.myCounter +=1
                        Label(SELF.bF,
                            text= SELF.myCounter).grid(column=2,row=1)
                    time.sleep(.3)
            except:
                    pass
```

```
def threadStart():
        dispTh=Thread(target=displayUPDATING, name='dispMSG',args=())
        dispTh.setDaemon(True)
        try:
                dispTh.start()
        except:
                print(sys.exc_info())
if __name__=="__main__":
        root = Tk()
        root.title("Button Press")
        root.geometry("300x230+1+10")#width, height, x location, y location
        Setup()
        threadStart()
        root.mainloop()
```

In the wiring diagram you will notice that the Cobbler was used on the breadboard. While you can wire this without the Cobbler, it sure makes life easier. You can also use your own wires vs the jumper wires.

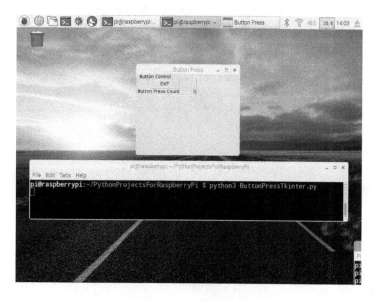

The wiring diagram uses the Cobbler **and note using 3.3V.** VERY IMPORTANT NOT TO EXCEED 3.3V AS INPUT TO GPIO PIN, YOU CAN EASILY FRY YOUR RASPBERRY IF VOLTAGE IS EXCEEDED.

A simple program, output to terminal. Run as python3 ButtonPressSimple.py If not working try to run as sudo python3 ButtonPressSimple.py as we are not using tkinker.
                              # ButtonPressSimple.py
```
import time
from time import sleep
import RPi.GPIO as GPIO
```

```python
GPIO.setmode(GPIO.BCM)
GPIO.setup(18, GPIO.IN, pull_up_down = GPIO.PUD_UP)
print("      to EXIT  press Ctrl + Z")
myCounter= 0
while True:
    try:
            myInputState = GPIO.input(18)
            if (myInputState ==0):    # False or zero
                print("Button Pressed myInputState = ",myInputState)
                time.sleep(.3)
                myCounter +=1
                print("Count: ",myCounter)
    except:
        pass
```

Tactile Switch/Button on Raspberry Pi

● Adafruit T-Cobbler Plus for Raspberry PI
Cobbler Plus on Breadboard

+	-		a	b	c	d	e		PIN #			f	g	h	i	j	k		+	-
								1	3v3	1	2	5.0v						1		
								2	SDA	3	4	5.0V						2		
								3	SCL	5	6	GND						3		
								4	#4	7	8	TXD						4		
								5	GND	9	10	RXD						5		
								6	#17	11	12	#18						6		
								7	#27	13	14	GND						7		
								8	#22	15	16	#23						8		
								9	3.3V	17	18	#24						9		
								10	MOSI	19	20	GND						10		
								11	MISO	21	22	#25						11		
								12	SCLK	23	24	CE0						12		
								13	GND	25	26	CD1						13		
								14	EED	27	28	EEC						14		
								15	#5	29	30	GND						15		
								16	#6	31	32	#12						16		
								17	#13	33	34	GND						17		
								18	#19	35	36	#16						18		
								19	#26	37	38	#20						19		
								20	GND	39	40	#21						20		
								21										21		
								22										22		
								23										23		
								24										24		
								25										25		
								26		V Out								26		
								27										27		
								28		V In								28		
								29										29		
								30										30		
			a	b	c	d	e					f	g	h	i	j	k			

Digital Clock

No wiring is needed for the project. Tkinter is used to display the time and date. A stop watch is included.

```python
#for python: 3.4.2 on Raspberry Pi                    DigitalClock.py
import timefrom time import sleep
from tkinter import *
from tkinter.ttk import *
import threading
from threading import Thread
import timeit


class SELF:
        pass                    # set up, define later as needed

def myStyle():
        SELF.S=Style()
        SELF.S.theme_use('classic')
        SELF.S.configure('e.TButton',font=('times 14 bold'),background="yellow")
        SELF.S.configure('c.TButton',font=('times 12 '), width = 15,padding=2)
        SELF.S.map('c.TButton',
                foreground=[('pressed','red'),('active','blue')],
                background=[('pressed','cyan'),('active','green')],
                relief=[('pressed','groove'),('!pressed','ridge')])

        SELF.S.configure('TLabel',font=('Times 12'),width=13,anchor=CENTER)
        SELF.S.configure('c.TLabel',relief='sunken',font=('Times 24'),width=18)

def Setup():
        bFrame=LabelFrame(root,text="Button Control",width=90,height=90)
        bFrame.grid(column=0,columnspan=3,row=0)
        Button(bFrame, text='EXIT',
                command=root.destroy,style='e.TButton').grid(column=0,row=0)
        Button(bFrame, text='Stop Watch', command=stopWatch).grid(column=1,row=0)
        SELF.dispSwitch= StringVar()
        SELF.dispSwitch.set('Display  ON')
        Button(bFrame, textvariable=SELF.dispSwitch,
                command=startDisp,style='c.TButton').grid(column=2,row=0)

def startDisp():
        if SELF.dispSwitch.get() == "Display  ON":
```

```python
                SELF.dispSwitch.set("Display OFF")
        else:
                SELF.dispSwitch.set("Display  ON")

def stopWatch():
        print("at time test")
        SELF.TOP=Toplevel()
        SELF.TOP.title("Stop Watch")
        SELF.TOP.geometry("305x150+245+140")#width, height, x location, y location
        Button(SELF.TOP,text="Exit",
                command=SELF.TOP.destroy).grid(column=0,row=0)
        Button(SELF.TOP,text="START",
                command=startStopWatch).grid(column=1,row=0)
        Button(SELF.TOP,text="STOP",
                command=stopStopWatch).grid(column=2,row=0)

def startStopWatch():
        SELF.startTime= timeit.default_timer()

def stopStopWatch():
        endTime= timeit.default_timer()
        elapTime = endTime-SELF.startTime
        msg = "Elap Time in Seconds:  " + str("{0:.4f}".format(elapTime))
        elapTime = str(msg)
        Label(SELF.TOP,text= elapTime,
                width=35).grid(column=0,columnspan=4,row=4)

def displayUPDATING():
        myTime= StringVar()
        while True:  #running via thread so can have control to stop it
                if SELF.dispSwitch.get()=="Display  ON":
                        baseTime = time.localtime(time.time())
                        temp=str(baseTime[3]) +":"+str(baseTime[4])+":"+str(baseTime[5])
                        myTime.set(temp)
                        Label(root,textvariable=myTime,
                                style='c.TLabel').grid(column=1,row =4)
                        myDate = "Date: "+str(baseTime[1])+"/"+ \
                                str(baseTime[2])+"/"+str(baseTime[0])
```

```
        Label(root,text=myDate,width=15,style='TLabel').grid(column=1,row=5)
            time.sleep(.1)        # value in seconds .1 seemed to work good

def threadStart():
    dispTh=Thread(target=displayUPDATING, name='dispMSG',args=())
    dispTh.setDaemon(True)
    try:
        dispTh.start()
    except:
        print(sys.exc_info())

if __name__=="__main__":
    root = Tk()
    root.title("Digital Clock and Stop Watch")
    root.geometry("400x130+1+10")#width, height, x location, y location
    myStyle()
    Setup()
    threadStart()
    root.mainloop()
```

Temperature

You will need to wire the breadboard and include the temperature sensor. Make sure you **use 3.3V.**

The temperature sensor does require MCP9808 library, a free download from Adafruit. This is the current location and instructions:

REQUIRES:

        MCP9808 Python Library

        cd ~

        git clone https://github.com/adafruit/Adafruit_Python_MCP9808.git

        cd Adafruit_Python_MCP98908

for python2   sudo python setup.py install

for python3   sudo python3 setup.py install

As we are using python3 that is the only install you need to run.

We are going to have several programs to run. The first will be the example included with the download.

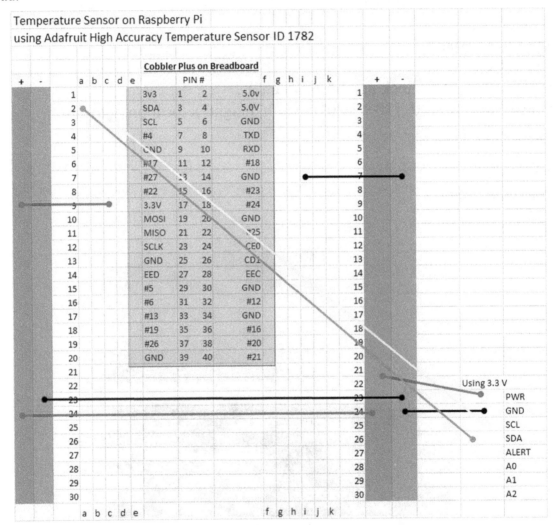

Run the sample included with the download from the directory you used for the download. In my case this was "/home/pi/Adafruit_Python_MCP9808/examples. Run the program python3 simpletest.py. If this does not work go back and install as python2 shown earlier. They try to run as python simpletest.py.

Once you have it running we can move on to more robust examples.

Temperature with LED

This program uses the basic example and adds a number of features.

```python
#!/usr/bin/python                          python3 temperatureTkinterLED.py
# Copyright (c) 2014 Adafruit Industries
# Author: Tony DiCola
# Permission is hereby granted, free of charge, to any person obtaining a copy
# of this software and associated documentation files (the "Software"), to deal
# in the Software without restriction, including without limitation the rights
# to use, copy, modify, merge, publish, distribute, sublicense, and/or sell
# copies of the Software, and to permit persons to whom the Software is
# furnished to do so, subject to the following conditions:
# The above copyright notice and this permission notice shall be included in
# all copies or substantial portions of the Software.
# THE SOFTWARE IS PROVIDED "AS IS", WITHOUT WARRANTY OF ANY KIND, EXPRESS
#OR IMPLIED, INCLUDING BUT NOT LIMITED TO THE WARRANTIES OF
#MERCHANTABILITY, FITNESS FOR A PARTICULAR PURPOSE AND NONINFRINGEMENT.
#IN NO EVENT SHALL THE AUTHORS OR COPYRIGHT HOLDERS BE LIABLE FOR ANY
#CLAIM, DAMAGES OR OTHER LIABILITY, WHETHER IN AN ACTION OF CONTRACT,
#TORT OR OTHERWISE, ARISING FROM, OUT OF OR IN CONNECTION WITH THE
#SOFTWARE OR THE USE OR OTHER DEALINGS IN THE SOFTWARE.

# 1/21/2017 Herb Norbom RyMax,Inc.
# using Python3: add class SELF, tkinter output and threading
# using GPIO for LED control

import time
from time import sleep
import Adafruit_MCP9808.MCP9808 as MCP9808

from tkinter import *
from tkinter.ttk import *
import threading
from threading import Thread
import RPi.GPIO as GPIO
GPIO.setmode(GPIO.BCM)

# Define a function to convert celsius to fahrenheit.
def c_to_f(c):
        return c * 9.0 / 5.0 + 32.0

sensor = MCP9808.MCP9808()
# Initialize communication with the sensor.
sensor.begin()
```

```python
class SELF:
        pass                    # set up, define later as needed

def myStyle():
        SELF.S=Style()
        SELF.S.theme_use('classic')
        SELF.S.configure('e.TButton',font=('times 14 bold'),background="yellow")
        SELF.S.configure('c.TButton',font=('times 12 '), width = 15,padding=2)
        SELF.S.map('c.TButton',
                foreground=[('pressed','red'),('active','blue')],
                background=[('pressed','cyan'),('active','green')],
                relief=[('pressed','groove'),('!pressed','ridge')])

        SELF.S.configure('TLabel',font=('Times 12'),width=15,anchor=E)
        SELF.S.configure('c.TLabel',relief='sunken',font=('Times 10'),
                width=20,foreground='green',anchor=CENTER)
        SELF.S.configure('d.TLabel',relief='raised',font=('Times 10'),
                width=45,foreground='red',anchor=CENTER)

def Setup():
        SELF.bFrame=LabelFrame(root,text="Button Control",width=90,height=90)
        SELF.bFrame.grid(column=0,columnspan=4,row=0,stick=W)
        Button(SELF.bFrame, text='EXIT',
                command=stopALL,style='e.TButton').grid(column=0,row=0)
        SELF.dispSwitch = StringVar()
        SELF.dispSwitch.set('STOP')
        Button(SELF.bFrame, textvariable=SELF.dispSwitch,
                command=startCount,style='e.TButton').grid(column=2,row=0)
        Label(root,text= "Farenheit",style='c.TLabel').grid(column=0,row=1)
        Label(root,text= "Centigrade",style='c.TLabel').grid(column=1,row=1)

def startCount():
        if SELF.dispSwitch.get() == "READ":
                SELF.dispSwitch.set("STOP")
        else:
                SELF.dispSwitch.set("READ")

def stopALL():
        GPIO.setup(18, GPIO.OUT)
```

```python
            sleep(.1)
            GPIO.cleanup()
            sleep(.1)
            root.destroy()


def displayUPDATING():
    while True:  #running via thread so can have control to stop
        if SELF.dispSwitch.get()=="READ":
            try:
                temp = sensor.readTempC()
                f=str('{:0.3F}'.format(c_to_f(temp)))
                Label(root,text=f).grid(column=0,row=2,sticky=W)
                c=str('{:0.3F}'.format(temp))
                Label(root,text=c).grid(column=1,row=2,sticky=W)
                sleep(1.0)
            except:
                print("Error on Read Sensor")
            if temp > 19.8:                         #adjust as needed
                GPIO.setup(18,GPIO.OUT)
                GPIO.output(18,True)
                sleep(.05)          #keep time low to lower LED burn out
                                    # add resistor if needed
                GPIO.output(18,False)
                l=Label(root,text="DANGER SAFE TEMP EXCEEDED",
                    width=34,style="d.TLabel")
                l.grid(column=0,columnspan=5,row=4, sticky=W)
                sleep(.5)
                l.grid_remove()


def threadStart():
    dispTh=Thread(target=displayUPDATING, name='dispMSG',args=())
    dispTh.setDaemon(True)
    try:
        dispTh.start()
    except:
        print(sys.exc_info())


if __name__=="__main__":
    root = Tk()
    root.title("Temperature Sensor")
```

```
root.geometry("300x230+1+10")#width, height, x location, y location
myStyle()
Setup()
threadStart()
root.mainloop()
```

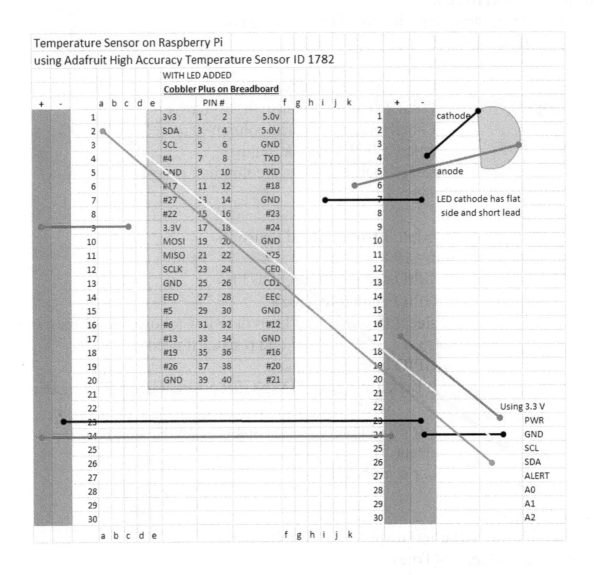

Temperature Sensor on Raspberry Pi
using Adafruit High Accuracy Temperature Sensor ID 1782

WITH LED ADDED

Cobbler Plus on Breadboard

+	-		a	b	c	d	e		PIN #			f	g	h	i	j	k		+	-		
			1					3v3	1	2	5.0v								1		cathode	
			2					SDA	3	4	5.0V								2			
			3					SCL	5	6	GND								3			
			4					#4	7	8	TXD								4			
			5					GND	9	10	RXD								5		anode	
			6					#17	11	12	#18								6			
			7					#27	13	14	GND								7		LED cathode has flat	
			8					#22	15	16	#23								8		side and short lead	
			9					3.3V	17	18	#24								9			
			10					MOSI	19	20	GND								10			
			11					MISO	21	22	#25								11			
			12					SCLK	23	24	CE0								12			
			13					GND	25	26	CD1								13			
			14					EED	27	28	EEC								14			
			15					#5	29	30	GND								15			
			16					#6	31	32	#12								16			
			17					#13	33	34	GND								17			
			18					#19	35	36	#16								18			
			19					#26	37	38	#20								19			
			20					GND	39	40	#21								20			
			21																21			
			22																22		Using 3.3 V	
			23																23		PWR	
			24																24		GND	
			25																25		SCL	
			26																26		SDA	
			27																27		ALERT	
			28																28		A0	
			29																29		A1	
			30																30		A2	

a b c d e   f g h i j k

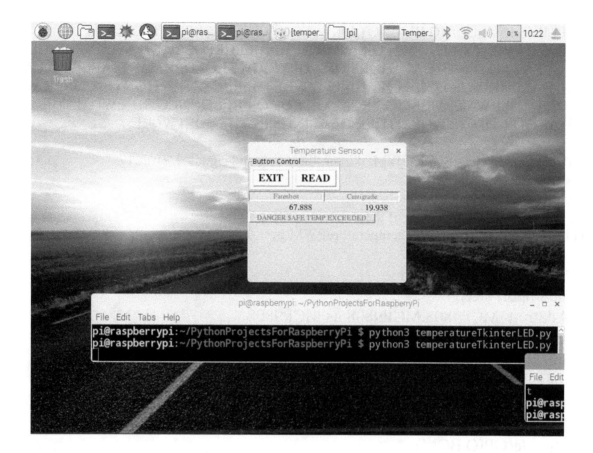

Temperature PWM control Fan

The program is similar to the previous one with some big exceptions. PWM is used to control a low voltage fan. My fan is running from the 3.3V on the Raspberry. The fan needs to draw minimal amperage. From what I can tell the maximum amperage varies depending on how many pins are drawing power. It would appear that below 16mA should be safe, but do some research.

This program will turn the fan on when temperature is above the level set in the program. The PWM will vary depending on how high the temperature is.

The program also uses signal (Ctrl + c) to stop the program if needed.

```
#!/usr/bin/python                          python3 temperatureTkinterPWM.py
# Copyright (c) 2014 Adafruit Industries
# Author: Tony DiCola
#
# Permission is hereby granted, free of charge, to any person obtaining a copy
# of this software and associated documentation files (the "Software"), to deal
# in the Software without restriction, including without limitation the rights
# to use, copy, modify, merge, publish, distribute, sublicense, and/or sell
# copies of the Software, and to permit persons to whom the Software is
# furnished to do so, subject to the following conditions:
# The above copyright notice and this permission notice shall be included in
# all copies or substantial portions of the Software.
# THE SOFTWARE IS PROVIDED "AS IS", WITHOUT WARRANTY OF ANY KIND, EXPRESS
```

```
# OR IMPLIED, INCLUDING BUT NOT LIMITED TO THE WARRANTIES OF
# MERCHANTABILITY, FITNESS FOR A PARTICULAR PURPOSE AND NONINFRINGEMENT.
# IN NO EVENT SHALL THE AUTHORS OR COPYRIGHT HOLDERS BE LIABLE FOR ANY
# CLAIM, DAMAGES OR OTHER LIABILITY, WHETHER IN AN ACTION OF CONTRACT,
# TORT OR OTHERWISE, ARISING FROM, OUT OF OR IN CONNECTION WITH THE
# SOFTWARE OR THE USE OR OTHER DEALINGS IN THE SOFTWARE.

# using Python3: add class SELF, PWM, tkinter, threading and signal  1/21/2017
# Herb Norbom RyMax,Inc.
# using GPIO for PWM control
# NOTE** tkinter will not work as of these versions using sudo
# if you have to use sudo run  sudo temperaturePWM.py

import time
from time import sleep
import Adafruit_MCP9808.MCP9808 as MCP9808
from tkinter import *
from tkinter.ttk import *
import threading
from threading import Thread
import RPi.GPIO as GPIO
GPIO.setmode(GPIO.BCM)
GPIO.setup(18,GPIO.IN)

import sys, signal
def signal_handler(signal, frame):#SO CTRL + C      CAN STOP PROGRAM
        print("signal exit, run stopALL")
        stopALL()
signal.signal(signal.SIGINT, signal_handler)

# Define a function to convert celsius to fahrenheit.
def c_to_f(c):
        return c * 9.0 / 5.0 + 32.0

sensor = MCP9808.MCP9808()
# Initialize communication with the sensor.
sensor.begin()

class SELF:
        pass               # set up, define later as needed
```

```python
def myStyle():
    SELF.S=Style()
    SELF.S.theme_use('classic')
    SELF.S.configure('e.TButton',font=('times 14 bold'),background="yellow")
    SELF.S.configure('c.TButton',font=('times 12 '), width = 15,padding=2)
    SELF.S.map('c.TButton',
        foreground=[('pressed','red'),('active','blue')],
        background=[('pressed','cyan'),('active','green')],
        relief=[('pressed','groove'),('!pressed','ridge')])

    SELF.S.configure('TLabel',font=('Times 12'),width=15,anchor=E)
    SELF.S.configure('c.TLabel',relief='sunken',font=('Times 10'),
        width=20,foreground='green',anchor=CENTER)
    SELF.S.configure('d.TLabel',relief='raised',font=('Times 10'),
        width=45,foreground='red',anchor=CENTER)

def Setup():
    SELF.bFrame=LabelFrame(root,text="Button Control",width=90,height=90)
    SELF.bFrame.grid(column=0,columnspan=4,row=0,stick=W)
    Button(SELF.bFrame, text='EXIT',
        command=stopALL,style='e.TButton').grid(column=0,row=0)
    SELF.dispSwitch = StringVar()
    SELF.dispSwitch.set('STOP')
    Button(SELF.bFrame, textvariable=SELF.dispSwitch,
        command=startCount,style='e.TButton').grid(column=2,row=0)
    Label(root,text= "Farenheit",style='c.TLabel').grid(column=0,row=1)
    Label(root,text= "Centigrade",style='c.TLabel').grid(column=1,row=1)
#pwm setup
    SELF.dc=80.0# Duty cycle % of time between pulses that signal is on/off
                    # range is 0.0 to 100.0,  100 is the highest power setting
    GPIO.setup(21, GPIO.LOW)   # pwm FAN Motor low voltage as running off
                            #GPIO Pin
    SELF.p21 = GPIO.PWM(21,100)      # channel and frequency
    SELF.p21.start(0)               # effective off
    GPIO.setup(21, GPIO.HIGH)

def startCount():
    if SELF.dispSwitch.get() == "READ":
        SELF.dispSwitch.set("STOP")
    else:
```

```python
                SELF.dispSwitch.set("READ")

def stopALL():
    try:
            GPIO.setup(21, GPIO.OUT)
    except:
            pass
    sleep(.1)
    GPIO.cleanup()
    sleep(.1)
    root.destroy()


def displayUPDATING():
    while True:  #running via thread so can have control to stop
            if SELF.dispSwitch.get()=="READ":
                    try:
                            temp = sensor.readTempC()
                            f=str('{:0.3F}'.format(c_to_f(temp)))
                            Label(root,text=f).grid(column=0,row=2,sticky=W)
                            c=str('{:0.3F}'.format(temp))
                            Label(root,text=c).grid(column=1,row=2,sticky=W)
                            sleep(1.0)
                    except:
                            print("Error on Read Sensor")
                    GPIO.setup(21, GPIO.HIGH)   # pwm FAN Motor low voltage as
running off GPIO Pin
                    if temp > 22.1:
                            l=Label(root,text="DANGER SAFE TEMP
                                    EXCEEDED",width=34,style="d.TLabel")
                            l.grid(column=0,columnspan=5,row=4, sticky=W)
                            SELF.dc = temp * 4.3
                            if SELF.dc > 99.9:
                                    SELF.dc = 100.0          #maxium pwm value
                            msg="PWM duty cycle: " + str('{:0.3F}'.format(SELF.dc))
                            ldc=Label(root,text=msg,width=25,style="d.TLabel")
                            ldc.grid(column=0,columnspan=2,row=5, sticky=W)

# use a low voltage and low milliamp motor as powering from GPIO
                            GPIO.setup(21, GPIO.LOW)
                            SELF.p21.ChangeDutyCycle(SELF.dc)#increase to run faster
```

```
                        sleep(1.5)
                        l.grid_remove()
                        ldc.grid_remove()

def threadStart():
        dispTh=Thread(target=displayUPDATING, name='dispMSG',args=())
        dispTh.setDaemon(True)
        try:
                dispTh.start()
        except:
                print(sys.exc_info())

if __name__=="__main__":
        root = Tk()
        root.title("Temperature Sensor PWM")
        root.geometry("370x230+1+10")#width, height, x location, y location
        myStyle()
        Setup()
        threadStart()
        root.mainloop()
```

I did not add a capacitor, it may help if you are having problems with the motor starting and drawing too much power.

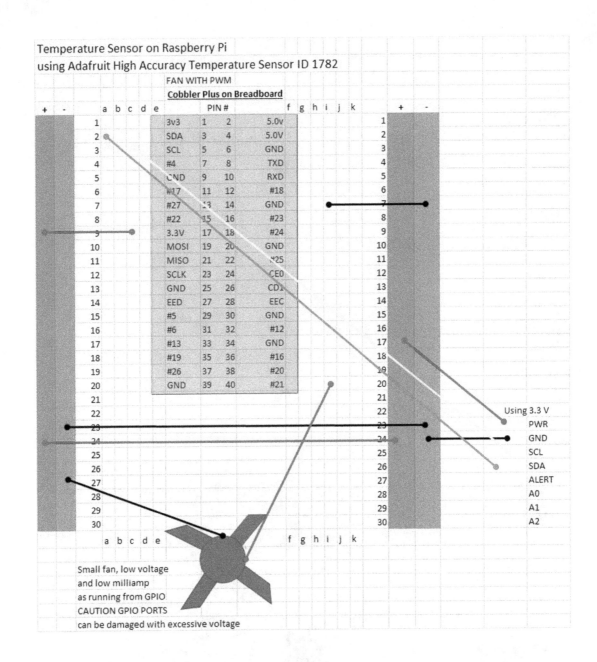

Temperature Sensor on Raspberry Pi
using Adafruit High Accuracy Temperature Sensor ID 1782

FAN WITH PWM

Cobbler Plus on Breadboard

Using 3.3 V
PWR
GND
SCL
SDA
ALERT
A0
A1
A2

Small fan, low voltage
and low milliamp
as running from GPIO
CAUTION GPIO PORTS
can be damaged with excessive voltage

If you are having problems running without sudo I have included this version without tkinter.

#!/usr/bin/python   python3 temperaturePWM.py

```
#!/usr/bin/python
# Copyright (c) 2014 Adafruit Industries
# Author: Tony DiCola
# Permission is hereby granted, free of charge, to any person obtaining a copy
# of this software and associated documentation files (the "Software"), to deal
# in the Software without restriction, including without limitation the rights
# to use, copy, modify, merge, publish, distribute, sublicense, and/or sell
# copies of the Software, and to permit persons to whom the Software is
# furnished to do so, subject to the following conditions:
# The above copyright notice and this permission notice shall be included in
```

```python
# all copies or substantial portions of the Software.
# THE SOFTWARE IS PROVIDED "AS IS", WITHOUT WARRANTY OF ANY KIND, EXPRESS
# OR IMPLIED, INCLUDING BUT NOT LIMITED TO THE WARRANTIES OF
# MERCHANTABILITY, FITNESS FOR A PARTICULAR PURPOSE AND NONINFRINGEMENT.
# IN NO EVENT SHALL THE AUTHORS OR COPYRIGHT HOLDERS BE LIABLE FOR ANY
# CLAIM, DAMAGES OR OTHER LIABILITY, WHETHER IN AN ACTION OF CONTRACT,
# TORT OR OTHERWISE, ARISING FROM, OUT OF OR IN CONNECTION WITH THE
# SOFTWARE OR THE USE OR OTHER DEALINGS IN THE SOFTWARE.

# using Python3:  1/22/2017
# Herb Norbom RyMax,Inc.
# using GPIO for PWM control

import time
from time import sleep
import Adafruit_MCP9808.MCP9808 as MCP9808
import RPi.GPIO as GPIO
GPIO.setmode(GPIO.BCM)

import sys, signal
def signal_handler(signal, frame):#SO CTRL +C CAN STOP PROGRAM
        print("signal exit, run stopALL")
        stopALL()
signal.signal(signal.SIGINT, signal_handler)

def stopALL():
        try:
                GPIO.cleanup()      # may get error if GPIO not used
        except:
                pass
        sleep(.1)
        sys.exit(0)

# Define a function to convert celsius to fahrenheit.
def c_to_f(c):
        return c * 9.0 / 5.0 + 32.0

sensor = MCP9808.MCP9808()
# Initialize communication with the sensor.
sensor.begin()

class SELF:
```

```python
        pass                    # set up, define later as needed
SELF.dc=80.0                    # Duty cycle % of time between pulses that signal is off
#                               # range is 0.0 to 100.0,  100 is the highest power setting
GPIO.setup(21, GPIO.LOW)    # pwm FAN Motor low voltage as running off GPIO Pin
SELF.p21 = GPIO.PWM(21,100)      # channel and frequency
SELF.p21.start(0)               # effective off
GPIO.setup(21, GPIO.HIGH)

def displayUPDATING():
    while True:
        try:
            temp = sensor.readTempC()
            print('Temp: {0:0.3F}*C / {1:0.3F}*F'.format(temp, c_to_f(temp)))
            sleep(1.0)          # read approx once every second
        except:
            print("Error on Read Sensor")
        GPIO.setup(21, GPIO.HIGH)   # pwm FAN Motor low voltage as running
                                    # off GPIO Pin

        if temp > 20.2:
            print("DANGER SAFE TEMP EXCEEDED")
            SELF.dc = temp * 4.3
            if SELF.dc > 99.9:
                SELF.dc = 100.0         #maxium pwm value
            print("PWM duty cycle: " + str('{:0.3F}'.format(SELF.dc)))
# use a low voltage and low milliamp motor as powering from GPIO
            GPIO.setup(21, GPIO.LOW)
            SELF.p21.ChangeDutyCycle(SELF.dc)#increase will run faster
            sleep(1.5)   # let motor run approx 1 and 1/2 seconds


if __name__=="__main__":
    print("Crtl + c   to stop program A NORMAL EXIT")
    print("Crtl + z   to stop program if above not working")
    sleep(2)
    displayUPDATING()
    mainloop()
```

Converting Integer to Hex and Binary

This is a simple program that takes advantage of the formatting options of python. Simple input of an integer with some error trapping. Displays the corresponding Hex and Binary values.

```python
# python3 convert integer to Hex and Binary          digitalToHexToBinary.py
# Herb Norbom, RyMax,Inc. 1/8/2017
from tkinter import *
from tkinter.ttk import *
import time
from time import sleep

class SELF:
        pass                    # set up, define later as needed
def Setup():
        Button(root, text='EXIT', command=root.destroy).grid(column=0,row=0)
        Label(root, text='Input Interger 0 to 256').grid(column=0,row=1)
        SELF.myEntry=Entry(root,width=5)
        SELF.myEntry.insert(0,5)#(position,value)inserts "5" at position zero
        SELF.myEntry.grid(column=0,row=2)
        SELF.myEntry.bind("<Return>", myValidation)
        SELF.myEntry.bind("<KP_Enter>", myValidation)
        SELF.myEntry.focus()

def myValidation(event):
        try:
                SELF.m1.grid_remove()
        except:
                pass                    # pass as not set up until error

        try:
                temp = int(SELF.myEntry.get())          #as myEntry is returned as
                                                        # string need to convert to integer
        except:
                SELF.m1 = Label(root,text="Invalid Entry")
                SELF.m1.grid(column=3,row=0)
                return

        if ((temp < 0) or (temp > 256)):
                SELF.m1 = Label(root,text="Out of Range")
                SELF.m1.grid(column=3,row=0)
                return

        Label(root,text="Decimal:").grid(column=1,row=2,sticky=W)
        Label(root, text=temp).grid(column=2,row=2,sticky=E)
```

```python
        tempH = hex(temp)
        Label(root,text="Hex:").grid(column=1,row=3,sticky=W)
        Label(root, text=tempH).grid(column=2,row=3,sticky=E)

        tempB = str(format(temp,'08b'))
        Label(root,text="Binary:").grid(column=1,row=4,sticky=W)
        Label(root, text=tempB).grid(column=2,row=4,sticky=E)

if __name__=="__main__":
        root=Tk()
        root.title("My Integer to Hex and Binary")
        root.geometry("505x110+1+10")#width, height, x location, y location
        Setup()
        mainloop()
```

Stop Python Program

Demonstrates the use of python signal and keyboard interrupt.   Program has a fail safe to stop after limited run.

```python
# run from cmd line          python stopPython.py  or python3 stopPython.py
# tested on Windows 10, Python 3.6.0 and 3.5.2
# tested on Raspberry PI 3, GNU/Linux, version 8, jessie
# Linux version 4.4.38-v7 with Python 3.4.2 and 2.7.9
# as of 1/23/2017  Herb Norbom RyMax,Inc.


import time
from time import sleep
import sys
import signal


def signal_handler(signal,frame):
        print("Signal: ", signal,' Frame: ',frame)
        print("using signal_handler, calling sys.exit()")
        #you can do other stuff here, comment out sys.exit
        #program continues until fail safe limt
        sys.exit()

#if you comment out the next line program will use except KeyboardInterrupt
signal.signal(signal.SIGINT, signal_handler)

def displayUPDATING():
    myCount=0
    try:
        while True:
            print(myCount)
            myCount +=1
            sleep(.3)
            if myCount > 30:
                print("at count limit exceeded, will exit loop")
                sys.exit()
    except KeyboardInterrupt:
        print("KEYBOARD EXCEPTION will end loop")
    print("LOOP Ended")

if __name__ =="__main__":
    print("Crtl + c   to stop program A NORMAL EXIT")
    print("Crtl + z   ON LINUX to stop program if above not working")
    sleep(2)
    displayUPDATING()
```

Ultra Sonic Sensor

This is a nice little device to use on a robot. The actual sensor I am using requires 5V input, some can run on 3.3V. BEWARE, if you are powering the sensor with 5V YOU MUST REDUCE voltage below the GPIO input level, 3.3V. The easiest method is to build a voltage divider using resistors. Once you have built the divider test the output voltage with a multi-meter. My calculations indicated that I would have an output voltage of 2.24, the actual was 2.24. The voltage in from the Raspberry Pi measured at 5.43. You can use different resistors, just keep voltage below safe level. Voltage calculator https://learn.sparkfun.com/tutorials/voltage-dividers if you don't want to do the math.

The program uses Tkinter and displays the distance in centimeters and inches.

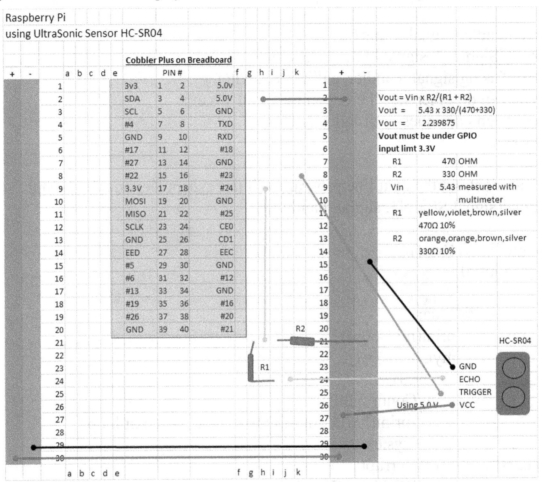

Raspberry Pi using UltraSonic Sensor HC-SR04

$$V_{out} = V_{in} \times R2/(R1 + R2)$$
$$V_{out} = 5.43 \times 330/(470+330)$$
$$V_{out} = 2.239875$$

Vout must be under GPIO input limt 3.3V

R1	470	OHM
R2	330	OHM
Vin	5.43	measured with multimeter
R1	yellow,violet,brown,silver	
	470Ω 10%	
R2	orange,orange,brown,silver	
	330Ω 10%	

```
#                                              python3 ultraSonicSensorTkinter.py
# Herb Norbom RyMax,Inc. 1/30/2017
import time
from time import sleep
from tkinter import *
from tkinter.ttk import *
import threading
```

```python
from threading import Thread
import RPi.GPIO as GPIO
GPIO.setmode(GPIO.BCM)
#GPIO.setwarnings(False)               #turn off GPIO warnings

import sys, signal
def signal_handler(signal, frame):     # SO CTRL + C  CAN STOP PROGRAM
    print("signal exit, run stopALL")  # if needed
    stopALL()
signal.signal(signal.SIGINT, signal_handler)

class SELF:
    pass               # set up, define later as needed

SELF.TRIG = 23         # BCM is 23 actual pin is 16
SELF.ECHO = 24         # BCM is 24 actual pin is 18

def myStyle():
    SELF.S=Style()
    SELF.S.theme_use('classic')
    SELF.S.configure('e.TButton',font=('times 14 ' ),background="yellow")
    SELF.S.configure('c.TButton',font=('times 12 '), width =15,padding=2)
    SELF.S.map('c.TButton',
        foreground=[('pressed','red'),('active','blue')],
        background=[('pressed','cyan'),('active','green')],
        relief=[('pressed','groove'),('!pressed','ridge')])

    SELF.S.configure('TLabel',font=('Times 12'),width=15,anchor=E)
    SELF.S.configure('c.TLabel',relief='sunken',font=('Times 10'),
        width=20,foreground='green',anchor=CENTER)
    SELF.S.configure('d.TLabel',relief='raised',font=('Times 10'),
        width=45,foreground='red',anchor=CENTER)
def Setup():
    SELF.bF=LabelFrame(root,text="Button Control",width=90,height=90)
    SELF.bF.grid(column=0,columnspan=4,row=0,stick=W)
    Button(SELF.bF, text='EXIT', command=stopALL,
        style='e.TButton').grid(column=0,row=0)
    SELF.dispSwitch = StringVar()
    SELF.dispSwitch.set('STOP')
    Button(SELF.bF, textvariable=SELF.dispSwitch,
```

```python
                    command=startCount,style='e.TButton').grid(column=2,row=0)
            Label(root,text= "Centimeter",style='c.TLabel').grid(column=0,row=1)
            Label(root,text= "Inch",style='c.TLabel').grid(column=1,row=1)


def startCount():
        if SELF.dispSwitch.get() == "READ":
                SELF.dispSwitch.set("STOP")
        else:
                SELF.dispSwitch.set("READ")


def stopALL():
        GPIO.cleanup()
        sleep(.1)
        root.destroy()


def displayUPDATING():
        while True:  #running via thread so can have control to stop
                if SELF.dispSwitch.get()=="READ":
                        try:
                                GPIO.setup(SELF.TRIG, GPIO.OUT)          #trigger
                                GPIO.setup(SELF.ECHO, GPIO.IN)           #echo
                                GPIO.output(SELF.TRIG, False)
                                sleep(0.5)
                                GPIO.output(SELF.TRIG, True)
                                sleep(0.00001)
                                GPIO.output(SELF.TRIG, False)
                                while GPIO.input(SELF.ECHO) == 0:
                                        start = time.time()
                                while GPIO.input(SELF.ECHO) == 1:
                                        stop = time.time()
                                elapsed = stop-start
                                distance = elapsed * 34321 / 2          #allow for round trip
                                                        # sound speed 343.21 meters/second
                                                        # sound speed 34,321 centimeters/second
                                distcm= '{0:.1f}'.format(distance)
                                Label(root,text=distcm).grid(column=0,row=2,sticky=W)
                                distance = distance *.393701     #convert to inch
                                distin= '{0:.1f}'.format(distance)
                                Label(root,text=distin).grid(column=1,row=2,sticky=W)
                                sleep(1.0)
```

```
                    except:
                            print("Error on Read Sensor")

def threadStart():
    dispTh=Thread(target=displayUPDATING, name='dispMSG',args=())
    dispTh.setDaemon(True)
    try:
            dispTh.start()
    except:
            print(sys.exc_info())

if __name__=="__main__":
    root = Tk()
    root.title("Ultrasonic Sensor Distance")
    root.geometry("370x230+1+10")#width, height, x location, y location
    myStyle()
    Setup()
    threadStart()
    root.mainloop()
```

Analog Thumb Joy Stick

Use a generic analog Thumb Joy Stick with two potentiometers. Move a square around the canvas with the Joy Stick. Convert analog Joy Stick to digital using Adafruit's analog to digital converter (ADS1015). The analog to digital device does need a FREE software download. Adafruit reference:

When downloading make sure you get the examples. See the wiring diagram that follows for more information on the installation of the software. Soldering is required for the device.

The Thumb Joy Stick is available from many sites. I purchased mine from MiniInTheBox. Prices vary widely, a good product search would be "Thumb JoyStick arduino".

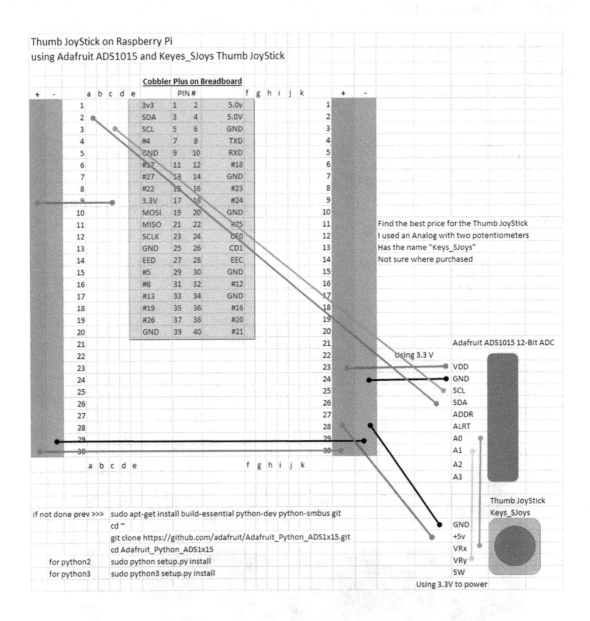

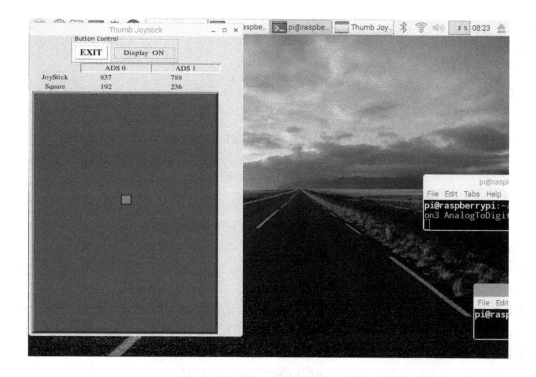

Simple demo of reading each analog input from the ADS1x15 and printing it to
the screen. Author: Tony DiCola License: Public Domain

#modified Herb Norbom, RyMax, Inc 2/1/2017   python3 AnalogToDigitalTkinter.py
#use python3 tkinter, threading. Move square around canvas by joystick display
# JoyStick values and square position on canvas
import time
from time import sleep
from tkinter import *
from tkinter.ttk import *
import threading
from threading import Thread

import Adafruit_ADS1x15   # Import the ADS1x15 module.
adc = Adafruit_ADS1x15.ADS1015() # Or create an ADS1015 ADC (12-bit) instance.

Note you can change the I2C address from its default (0x48), and/or the I2C
bus by passing in these optional parameters:
#adc = Adafruit_ADS1x15.ADS1015(address=0x49, busnum=1)

Choose a gain of 1 for reading voltages from 0 to 4.09V.
Or pick a different gain to change the range of voltages that are read:
- 2/3 = +/-6.144V

```python
#  -   1 = +/-4.096V
#  -   2 = +/-2.048V
#  -   4 = +/-1.024V
#  -   8 = +/-0.512V
#  -  16 = +/-0.256V
# See table 3 in the ADS1015/ADS1115 data sheet for more info on gain.
GAIN = 1


class SELF:
        pass                       # set up, define later as needed
def myStyle():
        SELF.S=Style()
        SELF.S.theme_use('classic')
        SELF.S.configure('e.TButton',font=('times 14 bold'),background="yellow")
        SELF.S.configure('c.TButton',font=('times 12 '), width = 15,padding=2)
        SELF.S.map('c.TButton',
                foreground=[('pressed','red'),('active','blue')],
                background=[('pressed','cyan'),('active','green')],
                relief=[('pressed','groove'),('!pressed','ridge')])
        SELF.S.configure('TLabel',font=('Times 12'),width=13,anchor=CENTER)
        SELF.S.configure('c.TLabel',relief='sunken',font=('Times 12'),width=18)


def Setup():
        bFrame=LabelFrame(root,text="Button Control",width=90,height=90)
        bFrame.grid(column=0,columnspan=3,row=0)
        Button(bFrame, text='EXIT', command=root.destroy,
                style='e.TButton').grid(column=0,row=0)
        SELF.dispSwitch= StringVar()
        SELF.dispSwitch.set('Display  ON')
        Button(bFrame, textvariable=SELF.dispSwitch, command=startDisp,
                style='c.TButton').grid(column=2,row=0)
        Label(root,text= "ADS 0",style='c.TLabel').grid(column=1,row=1)
        Label(root,text= "ADS 1",style='c.TLabel').grid(column=2,row=1)
        Label(root,text= "JoyStick",style='.TLabel').grid(column=0,row=2)
        Label(root,text= "Square",style='.TLabel').grid(column=0,row=3)
        SELF.Canvas=Canvas(root,width=385,height=540,borderwidth=5,
                relief=RAISED,background="blue")
        SELF.Canvas.grid(column=0,columnspan=4,row=4)
        SELF.star = SELF.Canvas.create_rectangle(182,260,202,280,fill="red")
```

```python
def startDisp():
    if SELF.dispSwitch.get() == "Display  ON":
        SELF.dispSwitch.set("Display OFF")
    else:
        SELF.dispSwitch.set("Display  ON")

def displayUPDATING():
    myTime= StringVar()
    while True: #running via thread so can have control to stop it
        if SELF.dispSwitch.get()=="Display  ON":
# Read all the ADC channel values in a list.
            values = [0]*2
            for i in range(2):
                values[i] = adc.read_adc(i, gain=GAIN)
            ads0=str('{:0}'.format(values[0]))
            Label(root,text=ads0).grid(column=1,row=2,sticky=W)
            ads1=str('{:0}'.format(values[1]))
            Label(root,text=ads1).grid(column=2,row=2,sticky=W)
            centX = values[0] - 645   # adjust to get to near center
            centY = values[1] - 552
            if centX > 368:                        # setup ranges to keep on canvas
                centX =368
            if centX < 5:
                centX =5
            if centY > 523:
                centY = 523
            if centY < 24:
                centY = 24
            Label(root,text=centX).grid(column=1,row=3,sticky=W)
            Label(root,text=centY).grid(column=2,row=3,sticky=W)
            time.sleep(0.1)
            SELF.Canvas.coords(SELF.star,centX,centY,centX+20,centY+20)

def threadStart():
    dispTh=Thread(target=displayUPDATING, name='dispMSG',args=())
    dispTh.setDaemon(True)
    try:
        dispTh.start()
    except:
        print(sys.exc_info())
```

```
if __name__=="__main__":
    root = Tk()
    root.title("Thumb Joystick")
    root.geometry("450x680+1+10")#width, height, x location, y location
    myStyle()
    Setup()
    threadStart()
    root.mainloop()
```

Servo Control

One of the best or easiest methods to control a servo or group of servos is with a control driver device. I am using Adafruit 16-Channel 12-bit PWM/Servo Driver – i2c interface PCA9685. While the Raspberry does have some PWM pins and Python can generate PWM, servos require somewhat specific timing. In addition with the PCA9685 you can support 16 servos. This does require you to download free software for the device. Download instructions included on the wiring diagram. I recommend that you check, https://learn.adafruit.com/adafruit-16-channel-servo-driver-with-raspberry-pi for possibly more current information. You will want to get the i2c-tools as this is a great help in configuring. The example program included with the download is a good test.

When you are ready to start your own program be aware that program Adafruit_PWM_Servo_Driver must be in your path. If you are developing in a separate directory copy the program to that directory. Good idea to copy the Adafruit_i2C.py also.

I am running a Micro Servo using 3.3V. The intention being to run with minimal voltage to minimize possible damage to the Raspberry.

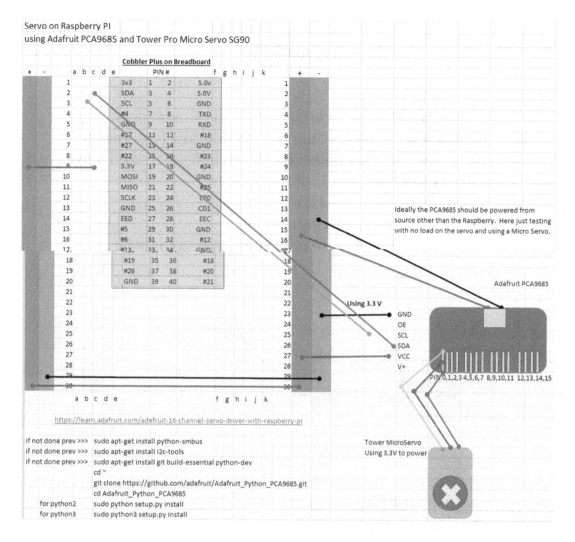

Servo on Raspberry PI
using Adafruit PCA9685 and Tower Pro Micro Servo SG90

```
#                                                    python3 servomove.py
# using Python 3.4.2   setup to run on Raspberry
# author Herb  2/1/2017  company RyMax, Inc. www.rymax.biz

from tkinter import *
from time import sleep
from Adafruit_PWM_Servo_Driver import PWM
import time

class SELF:        #define as needed
    pass
SELF.servoMin =150              # Min pulse length out of 4096
SELF.servoMax = 600     # Max pulse length out of 4096
SELF.servoCen = 375              # Center pulse length out of 4096
```

```python
pwm = PWM(0x40)                    # Initialise the PWM device using the default address
pwm.setPWMFreq(60)   # Set frequency to 60 Hz

def mRight():
        # servo on channel O, On/Off Tick(0-4095),to mimimum position
        # if using the Tick start and stop, stop will replace SELF.servoMin.
        # Controls the amount of time power on.  Keep at 0 unless you know
        # how it works.  Beyond the scope of this example.
        pwm.setPWM(0, 0, SELF.servoMin)
        SELF.servoPosition = SELF.servoMin
        Label(root, text=SELF.servoPosition).grid(column=3,row=5)
        time.sleep(.5)

def mLeft():
 # servo on channel O, On/Off Tick(0-4095), position to maximum
        pwm.setPWM(0, 0, SELF.servoMax)
        SELF.servoPosition = SELF.servoMax
        Label(root, text=SELF.servoPosition).grid(column=3,row=5)
        time.sleep(.5)

def mCenter():
 # servo on channel O, On/Off Tick(0-4095), to center position
        pwm.setPWM(0, 0, SELF.servoCen)
        SELF.servoPosition = SELF.servoCen
        Label(root, text=SELF.servoPosition).grid(column=3,row=5)
        time.sleep(.5)

def sLeft():
 # servo on channel O, On/Off Tick(0-4095),  to step left 35 position
        newPosition = SELF.servoPosition +35
        if newPosition > SELF.servoMax:
                newPosition = SELF.servoMax

        pwm.setPWM(0, 0,newPosition)
        SELF.servoPosition = newPosition
        Label(root, text=SELF.servoPosition).grid(column=3,row=5)
        time.sleep(.5)

def sRight():
 # servo on channel O, On/Off Tick(0-4095),  to step right 35 position
```

```python
            newPosition = SELF.servoPosition -35
            if newPosition < SELF.servoMin:
                    newPosition = SELF.servoMin
            pwm.setPWM(0, 0,newPosition)
            SELF.servoPosition = newPosition
            Label(root, text=SELF.servoPosition).grid(column=3,row=5)
            time.sleep(.5)

def callEXIT():
        print("program stop ordered")        # display on console
        try:
                root.destroy()                #close tkinter windows
        except:
                print ('error on stop')

def Setup():
        Button(root, text="< Left", fg='green',
                command=mLeft).grid(column=2, row=1)
        Button(root, text="Center", fg='blue',
                command=mCenter).grid(column=3, row=1)
        Button(root, text="Right>", fg='red',
                command=mRight).grid(column=4, row=1)
        Button(root, text="Step 35 Left", fg='green',
                command=sLeft).grid(column=2, row=2)
        Button(root, text="Step 35 Right", fg='red',
                command=sRight).grid(column=4, row=2)
        Button(root, text="EXIT", fg='red',
                command=callEXIT).grid(column=1, row=4,sticky=(W))
        Label(root, text="Servo Position").grid(column=2, row =5)
# move servo to center to establish reference and startup position
        mCenter()

if __name__ == '__main__':
        root = Tk()
        root.title("Servo Control")
        root.geometry("330x230+1+10")#width, height, x location, y location
        Setup()
        root.mainloop()
```

Stepper Motor Control

Stepper motors are very interesting and can be complex. In my example I am using a low voltage stepper. I am using an H-Bridge for control and I am powering the stepper from the Raspberry 5.0V. While it is usually better to use a separate power source I am not going to because the Raspberry can be easily damaged with excess voltage. You also need to be aware that the Raspberry power fuse can be blown with excessive power drain, as heat limits appear to be exceeded. I suggest you keep run times low and do not put a lot of load on the stepper. The tutorials on Adafruit are a good reference site for getting familiar with the concepts.

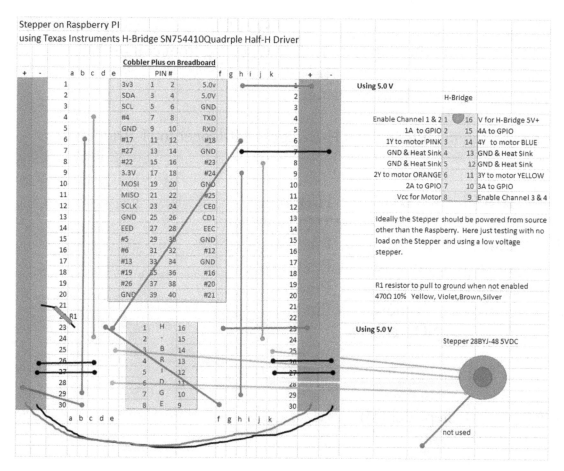

Stepper on Raspberry PI
using Texas Instruments H-Bridge SN754410Quadrple Half-H Driver

Using 5.0 V

H-Bridge

Enable Channel 1 & 2	1		16	V for H-Bridge 5V+
1A to GPIO	2		15	4A to GPIO
1Y to motor PINK	3		14	4Y to motor BLUE
GND & Heat Sink	4		13	GND & Heat Sink
GND & Heat Sink	5		12	GND & Heat Sink
2Y to motor ORANGE	6		11	3Y to motor YELLOW
2A to GPIO	7		10	3A to GPIO
Vcc for Motor	8		9	Enable Channel 3 & 4

Ideally the Stepper should be powered from source
other than the Raspberry. Here just testing with no
load on the Stepper and using a low voltage
stepper.

R1 resistor to pull to ground when not enabled
470Ω 10% Yellow, Violet, Brown, Silver

Using 5.0 V

Stepper 28BYJ-48 5VDC

not used

```
#                                                python3 stepperpython3.py
# using Python 3.4.2   setup to run on Raspberry
# author Herb  2/9/2017  company RyMax, Inc. www.rymax.biz
# set for half or full step, set time delay between pulses,
# set number of steps to run
import time
from time import sleep
from tkinter import *
from tkinter.ttk import *
import tkinter.messagebox
import threading
from threading import Thread
import RPi.GPIO as GPIO
GPIO.setmode(GPIO.BCM)
GPIO.setwarnings(False)

import sys
import signal
```

```python
def signal_handler(signal, frame):          # SO CTRL + C  CAN STOP PROGRAM
        print("signal exit, run stopALL")    # if needed from command line
        stopALL()
signal.signal(signal.SIGINT, signal_handler)

#stepper coil assign to GPIO pin via H-Bridge, and stepper to H-Bridge
#adjust as needed

#       GPIO H-Bridge     28BYJ-48   H-Bridge
# ***************      ********************
A1 = 4  #   Pin 2        pink       Pin    3
A2 = 17 #   Pin 6        orange     Pin 6
B1 = 23 #   Pin 15       blue       Pin 14
B2 = 24 #   Pin 10       yellow     Pin 11
            #        red NOT USED

#four STEP or FULL STEP  works with 28BYJ-48
StepCount4 = 4
Seq4 = list(range(0, StepCount4))
Seq4[0] = [1,0,1,0]
Seq4[1] = [0,1,1,0]
Seq4[2] = [0,1,0,1]
Seq4[3] = [1,0,0,1]

# 8 STEP or HALF STEP works with 28BYJ-48 5VDC
StepCount8 = 8
Seq8 = list(range(0, StepCount8))
Seq8[0] = [0,1,0,0]
Seq8[1] = [0,1,0,1]
Seq8[2] = [0,0,0,1]
Seq8[3] = [1,0,0,1]
Seq8[4] = [1,0,0,0]
Seq8[5] = [1,0,1,0]
Seq8[6] = [0,0,1,0]
Seq8[7] = [0,1,1,0]

GPIO.setup(A1, GPIO.OUT)
GPIO.setup(A2, GPIO.OUT)
GPIO.setup(B1, GPIO.OUT)
GPIO.setup(B2, GPIO.OUT)
```

```python
def setStep(w1, w2, w3, w4):
    GPIO.output(A1, w1)             #GPIO pin and on/off from Seq
    GPIO.output(A2, w2)
    GPIO.output(B1, w3)
    GPIO.output(B2, w4)


def forward():
    delay = float(SELF.myDelay) / 1000.0
    if SELF.FullorHalf == 4:
        for i in range(SELF.myNumSteps):
            for j in range(StepCount4):
                setStep(Seq4[j][0], Seq4[j][1], Seq4[j][2], Seq4[j][3])
                sleep(delay)
    if SELF.FullorHalf == 8:
        for i in range(SELF.myNumSteps):
            for j in range(StepCount8):
                setStep(Seq8[j][0], Seq8[j][1], Seq8[j][2], Seq8[j][3])
                sleep(delay)


def backwards():
    delay = float(SELF.myDelay) / 1000.0
    if SELF.FullorHalf ==4:
        for i in range(SELF.myNumSteps):
            for j in reversed(range(StepCount4)):
                setStep(Seq4[j][0], Seq4[j][1], Seq4[j][2], Seq4[j][3])
                sleep(delay)
    if SELF.FullorHalf ==8:
        for i in range(SELF.myNumSteps):
            for j in reversed(range(StepCount8)):
                setStep(Seq8[j][0], Seq8[j][1], Seq8[j][2], Seq8[j][3])
                sleep(delay)
class SELF:
    pass                   # set up, define later as needed


SELF.myDelay = 4.1         # default time between steps
SELF.myNumSteps = 20       # default number of steps to move
SELF.FullorHalf = 8        # default step selection either 4 or 8
        # 8 step can run at a lower delay than 4 step
        # if delay is too low stepper will not move
```

```python
# for smoother run use 8 step. Delay as low as possible, maybe a 2.
# Seems to run a little smoother in one direction vs the other.

class self:
    pass                    # set up, define later as needed

def myStyle():
    SELF.S=Style()
    SELF.S.theme_use('classic')
    SELF.S.configure('e.TButton',font=('times 14 bold'),background="yellow")
    SELF.S.configure('c.TButton',font=('times 12 '), width = 15,padding=2)
    SELF.S.map('c.TButton',
        foreground=[('pressed','red'),('active','blue')],
        background=[('pressed','cyan'),('active','green')],
        relief=[('pressed','groove'),('!pressed','ridge')])

    SELF.S.configure('TLabel',font=('Times 12'),width=25,anchor=W)
    SELF.S.configure('c.TLabel',relief='sunken',font=('Times 10'),
        width=40,foreground='green',anchor=CENTER)
    SELF.S.configure('d.TLabel',relief='raised',font=('Times 10'),
        width=45,foreground='red',anchor=CENTER)

def Setup():
    SELF.bF=LabelFrame(root,text="Button Control",width=90,height=90)
    SELF.bF.grid(column=0,columnspan=4,row=0,stick=W)
    Button(SELF.bF, text='EXIT', command=stopALL,
        style='e.TButton').grid(column=0,row=0)

    SELF.EnableSwitch = StringVar()
    SELF.EnableSwitch.set('DISABLE H-Bridge')

    Button(SELF.bF, textvariable=SELF.EnableSwitch, command=ENABLE,
        style='e.TButton').grid(column=1,columnspan=2,row=0)

    Button(SELF.bF,text= "Run Stepper",command=runStepper,
            width=20).grid(column=0,row=1)

    SELF.dispSwitch = StringVar()
    SELF.dispSwitch.set('STOP')
    Button(SELF.bF, textvariable=SELF.dispSwitch,
```

```python
            command=startRun,style='e.TButton').grid(column=2,row=1)
        Label(root,text= "Time Between Steps:",
            style='TLabel').grid(column=0,row=1)
        msg = "A delay of 5.1 will be 0.0050999999"
        Label(root,text= msg,
            style='c.TLabel').grid(column=0,columnspan=2,row=6)
        Label(root,text= "Number of Steps:",
            style='TLabel').grid(column=0,row=2)
        Label(root,text= "Four Step=4 or Eight Step=8:",
            style='TLabel').grid(column=0,row=3)

        self.myDelay=Entry(root, width=4)
        self.myDelay.insert(0, SELF.myDelay)
        self.myDelay.bind("<Return>", validate)
        self.myDelay.bind("<KP_Enter>", validate)
        self.myDelay.grid(column=1,row=1)
        self.myDelay.focus()

        self.myNumSteps=Entry(root, width=4)
        self.myNumSteps.insert(0, SELF.myNumSteps)
        self.myNumSteps.bind("<Return>", validate)
        self.myNumSteps.bind("<KP_Enter>", validate)
        self.myNumSteps.grid(column=1,row=2)
        self.myNumSteps.focus()

        self.FullorHalf=Entry(root, width=4)
        self.FullorHalf.insert(0, SELF.FullorHalf)
        self.FullorHalf.bind("<Return>", validate)
        self.FullorHalf.bind("<KP_Enter>", validate)
        self.FullorHalf.grid(column=1,row=3)
        self.FullorHalf.focus()

        Button(root,text='Validate',command=lambda c=0:validate(c),
            width=20).grid(column=0,row=5)
def validate(event):
    try:
            SELF.myDelay=float(self.myDelay.get())
    except:
            tkinter.messagebox.showwarning("Time Between Steps","Enter an \
                Integer or Decimal for delay")
```

```python
                self.myDelay.focus()
                return

        try:
                SELF.myNumSteps=int(self.myNumSteps.get())
        except:
                tkinter.messagebox.showwarning("Number of Steps",
                        "Enter an Integer for number of steps")
                self.myNumSteps.focus()
                return

        try:
                SELF.FullorHalf=int(self.FullorHalf.get())
        except:
                tkinter.messagebox.showwarning("Half or Full Step",
                        "Enter an Integer for Half=8 or Full=4")
                self.FullorHalf.focus()
                return
        if ((SELF.FullorHalf == 4) or (SELF.FullorHalf == 8)):
                pass
        else:
                tkinter.messagebox.showwarning("Invalid Half or Full",
                        "Enter 4 or 8")
                self.FullorHalf.focus()
                return

def ENABLE():
        if SELF.EnableSwitch.get() =='ENABLE H-Bridge':
                SELF.EnableSwitch.set('DISABLE H-Bridge')
                enable_pin = 18
                GPIO.output(enable_pin, 0)
        else:
                SELF.EnableSwitch.set('ENABLE H-Bridge')
                enable_pin = 18
                GPIO.setup(enable_pin, GPIO.OUT)
                GPIO.output(enable_pin, 1)

def startRun():
        if SELF.dispSwitch.get() == "RUN":
                SELF.dispSwitch.set("STOP")
```

```
        else:
            SELF.dispSwitch.set("RUN")

def runStepper():
    forward()
    sleep(1)
    backwards()
    setStep(0,0,0,0)

def stopALL():
    GPIO.cleanup()
    sleep(.1)
    root.destroy()

def displayUPDATING():
    setStep(0,0,0,0)              # effective stepper off
    while True:  #running via thread so can have control to stop
        if SELF.dispSwitch.get()=="RUN":
            try:
                forward()
                sleep(1)
                backwards()
                setStep(0,0,0,0)            # effective stepper off
                sleep(3)
            except:
                print("Error on Stepper")

def threadStart():
    dispTh=Thread(target=displayUPDATING, name='dispMSG',args=())
    dispTh.setDaemon(True)
    try:
        dispTh.start()
    except:
        print(sys.exc_info())

if __name__=="__main__":
    root = Tk()
    root.title("Stepper Motor Control")
    root.geometry("450x230+1+10")#width, height, x location, y location
    myStyle()
```

```
Setup()
threadStart()
root.mainloop()
```

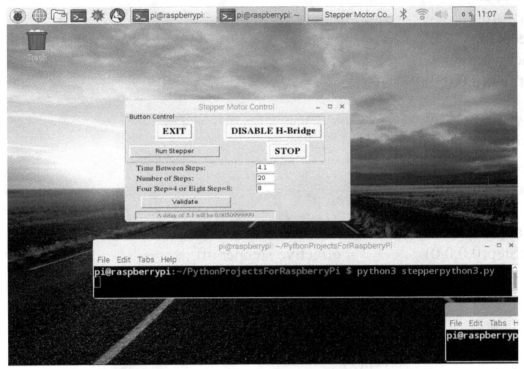

Color Sensor

This program displays the digital and hex values of the color detected. A fairly close representation of the color is displayed on a canvas widget. I found that the LED needs to be on and the sensor works best about ¼ inch from the target. You will need to get the FREE download for the Adafruit TCS34725. Available at https://github.com/adafruit/Adafruit_Python_TCS34725 See the wiring diagram for installation.

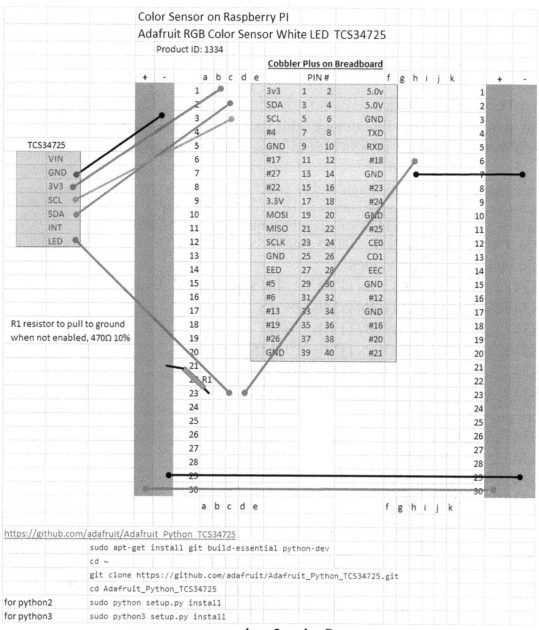

Color Sensor on Raspberry PI
Adafruit RGB Color Sensor White LED TCS34725
Product ID: 1334

https://github.com/adafruit/Adafruit_Python_TCS34725

```
sudo apt-get install git build-essential python-dev
cd ~
git clone https://github.com/adafruit/Adafruit_Python_TCS34725.git
cd Adafruit_Python_TCS34725
```

for python2	`sudo python setup.py install`
for python3	`sudo python3 setup.py install`

```
#                    python3 colorSensor.py
#using Adafruit TCS34725, based on Tony DiCola test program
# using Python 3.4.2   setup to run on Raspberry
# author Herb  2/13/2017  company RyMax, Inc. www.rymax.biz
import time
from time import sleep
from tkinter import *
from tkinter.ttk import *
import threading
from threading import Thread
import RPi.GPIO as GPIO
```

```
GPIO.setmode(GPIO.BCM)

# Import the TCS34725 module.
import Adafruit_TCS34725
# Create a TCS34725 instance with default integration time (2.4ms) and gain (4x).
# You can also override the I2C device address and/or bus with parameters:
#tcs = Adafruit_TCS34725.TCS34725(address=0x30, busnum=2)

# Or you can change the integration time and/or gain:
# uncomment next TWO lines to use 700ms and gain of 60 for example
#tcs = Adafruit_TCS34725.TCS34725(integration_time=Adafruit_TCS34725.\
#TCS34725_INTEGRATIONTIME_700MS,gain=Adafruit_TCS34725.TCS34725_GAIN_60X)
# Possible integration time values:
#  - TCS34725_INTEGRATIONTIME_2_4MS  (2.4ms, default)
#  - TCS34725_INTEGRATIONTIME_24MS
#  - TCS34725_INTEGRATIONTIME_50MS
#  - TCS34725_INTEGRATIONTIME_101MS
#  - TCS34725_INTEGRATIONTIME_154MS
#  - TCS34725_INTEGRATIONTIME_700MS
# Possible gain values:
#  - TCS34725_GAIN_1X
#  - TCS34725_GAIN_4X
#  - TCS34725_GAIN_16X
#  - TCS34725_GAIN_60X

import smbus

class SELF:
        pass                 # set up, define later as needed
SELF.tcs = Adafruit_TCS34725.TCS34725()

# Disable interrupts (can enable them by passing true,
#   see the set_interrupt_limits function too).
#tcs.set_interrupt(False)

import sys
import signal
def signal_handler(signal, frame):         # SO CTRL + C  CAN STOP PROGRAM
        print("signal exit, run stopALL")  # if needed from command line
        stopALL()
```

```
signal.signal(signal.SIGINT, signal_handler)

def myStyle():
    SELF.S=Style()
    SELF.S.theme_use('classic')
    SELF.S.configure('e.TButton',font=('times 14 bold'),background="yellow")
    SELF.S.configure('c.TButton',font=('times 12 '), width = 15,padding=2)
    SELF.S.map('c.TButton',
        foreground=[('pressed','red'),('active','blue')],
        background=[('pressed','cyan'),('active','green')],
        relief=[('pressed','groove'),('!pressed','ridge')])

    SELF.S.configure('TLabel',font=('Times 12'),width=25,anchor=W)
    SELF.S.configure('c.TLabel',relief='sunken',font=('Times 10'),
        width=40,foreground='green',anchor=CENTER)
    SELF.S.configure('d.TLabel',relief='raised',font=('Times 10'),
        width=45,foreground='red',anchor=CENTER)

def Setup():
    SELF.bF=LabelFrame(root,text="Button Control",width=90,height=90)
    SELF.bF.grid(column=0,columnspan=4,row=0,stick=W)
    Button(SELF.bF, text='EXIT', command=stopALL,
        style='e.TButton').grid(column=0,row=0)
    SELF.dispSwitch = StringVar()
    SELF.dispSwitch.set('STOP')
    Button(SELF.bF, textvariable=SELF.dispSwitch,
        command=startRun,style='e.TButton').grid(column=2,row=1)

    SELF.EnableSwitch = StringVar()
    SELF.EnableSwitch.set('LED OFF')
    Button(SELF.bF, textvariable=SELF.EnableSwitch, command=ENABLE,
        style='e.TButton').grid(column=0,columnspan=3,row=4,sticky=W)

    SELF.Canvas=Canvas(root, width =100, height=100, borderwidth=5,
        relief=RAISED)
    SELF.Canvas.grid(column=0,columnspan=3,row=2)

def startRun():
    if SELF.dispSwitch.get() == "RUN":
        SELF.dispSwitch.set("STOP")
```

```python
        else:
                SELF.dispSwitch.set("RUN")

def displayUPDATING():
        SELF.coloR = 17                #arbitrary starting values
        SELF.coloG = 12
        SELF.coloB = 36
        SELF.coloC = 100
        SELF.color_temp =1000
        SELF.lux = 500

        SELF.dF=LabelFrame(root,text="Color Information",width=90,height=90)
        SELF.dF.grid(column=5,row=0,stick=W)
        Label(SELF.dF,text="R ",style='TLabel',width=4).grid(column=1,row=0)
        Label(SELF.dF,text="G ",style='TLabel',width=4).grid(column=2,row=0)
        Label(SELF.dF,text="B ",style='TLabel',width=4).grid(column=3,row=0)
        Label(SELF.dF,text="C ",style='TLabel',width=4).grid(column=4,row=0)
#decimal values
        Label(SELF.dF,text="Decimal:",style='TLabel',width=11).grid(column=0,row=1)
        SELF.dR = StringVar()
        SELF.dR.set(str(SELF.coloR))
        L1=Label(SELF.dF,textvariable=SELF.dR, width=4)
        L1.grid(column=1,row=1)

        SELF.dG = StringVar()
        SELF.dG.set(str(SELF.coloG))
        Label(SELF.dF,textvariable=SELF.dG, width=4).grid(column=2,row=1)

        SELF.dB = StringVar()
        SELF.dB.set(str(SELF.coloB))
        Label(SELF.dF,textvariable=SELF.dB, width=4).grid(column=3,row=1)

        SELF.dC = StringVar()
        SELF.dC.set(str(SELF.coloC))
        Label(SELF.dF,textvariable=SELF.dC, width=4).grid(column=4,row=1)

#hex values
        Label(SELF.dF,text="Hex:",style='TLabel',width=11).grid(column=0,row=2)
        SELF.hexR = '{0:02x}'.format(SELF.coloR)
        SELF.hexG = '{0:02x}'.format(SELF.coloG)
```

```python
        SELF.hexB = '{0:02x}'.format(SELF.coloB)
        SELF.hexC = '{0:02x}'.format(SELF.coloC)


        SELF.hR = StringVar()
        SELF.hR.set(str(SELF.hexR))
        Label(SELF.dF,textvariable=SELF.hR, width=4).grid(column=1,row=2)

        SELF.hG = StringVar()
        SELF.hG.set(str(SELF.hexG))
        Label(SELF.dF,textvariable=SELF.hG, width=4).grid(column=2,row=2)

        SELF.hB = StringVar()
        SELF.hB.set(str(SELF.hexB))
        Label(SELF.dF,textvariable=SELF.hB, width=4).grid(column=3,row=2)

        SELF.hC = StringVar()
        SELF.hC.set(str(SELF.hexC))
        Label(SELF.dF,textvariable=SELF.hC, width=4).grid(column=4,row=2)

        Label(SELF.dF,text="Color Hex:", style='TLabel', width=11).grid(column=0,
            row=3)
        myColor="#"+str(SELF.hexR)+str(SELF.hexG)+str(SELF.hexB)
        SELF.myColor= StringVar()
        SELF.myColor.set("#"+str(SELF.hexR)+str(SELF.hexG)+str(SELF.hexB))
        Label(SELF.dF,textvariable=SELF.myColor, width=16).grid(column=1,\
            columnspan=2,row=3)
        Label(SELF.dF,text="Color Temp:",style='TLabel',width=11).grid(column=0,
            row=4)
        SELF.dColorTemp = StringVar()
        SELF.dColorTemp.set(str(SELF.color_temp))
        Label(SELF.dF,textvariable=SELF.dColorTemp,width=6).grid(column=1,row=4)

        Label(SELF.dF,text="Lux:",style='TLabel',width=11).grid(column=0,row=5)
        SELF.dLux = StringVar()
        SELF.dLux.set(str(SELF.lux))
        Label(SELF.dF,textvariable=SELF.dLux, width=6).grid(column=1,row=5)

        SELF.myOval=SELF.Canvas.create_oval(25,50,90,90,fill=myColor,
            outline=myColor)
        while True: #running via thread so can have control to stop
```

```python
        if SELF.dispSwitch.get()=="RUN":
            try:
                # Read the R, G, B, C color data.
                SELF.coloR, SELF.coloG, SELF.coloB, \
                    SELF.coloC = SELF.tcs.get_raw_data()

                # Calculate color temperature using utility functions.
#next 3 lines are one line of code, print format is not working well
                SELF.color_temp = \
        Adafruit_TCS34725.calculate_color_temperature(SELF.coloR, \
                    SELF.coloG, SELF.coloB)

                # Calculate lux with another utility function.
                SELF.lux = Adafruit_TCS34725.calculate_lux(SELF.coloR,
                    SELF.coloG, SELF.coloB)

                updateColors()
                sleep(.5)
            except:
                print("Error on Color Sensor")

def updateColors():
    if SELF.coloR > 255:
        SELF.coloR = 255
    if SELF.coloG > 255:
        SELF.coloG = 255
    if SELF.coloB > 255:
        SELF.coloB = 255
    SELF.dR.set(SELF.coloR)
    SELF.dG.set(SELF.coloG)
    SELF.dB.set(SELF.coloB)
    SELF.dC.set(SELF.coloC)
    SELF.hexR = '{0:02x}'.format(SELF.coloR)
    SELF.hexG = '{0:02x}'.format(SELF.coloG)
    SELF.hexB = '{0:02x}'.format(SELF.coloB)
    SELF.hexC = '{0:02x}'.format(SELF.coloC)
    SELF.hR.set(str(SELF.hexR))
    SELF.hG.set(str(SELF.hexG))
    SELF.hB.set(str(SELF.hexB))
    SELF.hC.set(str(SELF.hexC))
```

```python
        SELF.dColorTemp.set(str(SELF.color_temp))
        SELF.dLux.set(str(SELF.lux))

        SELF.myColor.set("#"+str(SELF.hexR)+str(SELF.hexG)+str(SELF.hexB))
        SELF.Canvas.itemconfig(SELF.myOval,fill=str(SELF.myColor.get()), \
            outline=str(SELF.myColor.get()))

def ENABLE():
    if SELF.EnableSwitch.get() =='LED ON':
        SELF.EnableSwitch.set('LED OFF')
        enable_pin = 18
        GPIO.output(enable_pin, 0)
    else:
        SELF.EnableSwitch.set('LED ON')
        enable_pin = 18
        GPIO.setup(enable_pin, GPIO.OUT)
        GPIO.output(enable_pin, 1)

def stopALL():
    GPIO.cleanup()
# Enable interrupts and put the chip back to low power sleep/disabled.
    SELF.tcs.set_interrupt(True)
    SELF.tcs.disable()
    sleep(.1)
    root.destroy()

def threadStart():
    dispTh=Thread(target=displayUPDATING, name='dispMSG',args=())
    dispTh.setDaemon(True)
    try:
        dispTh.start()
    except:
        print(sys.exc_info())

if __name__=="__main__":
    root = Tk()
    root.title("Color Sensor")
    root.geometry("470x270+1+10")#width, height, x location, y location
    myStyle()
```

```
Setup()
threadStart()
root.mainloop()
```

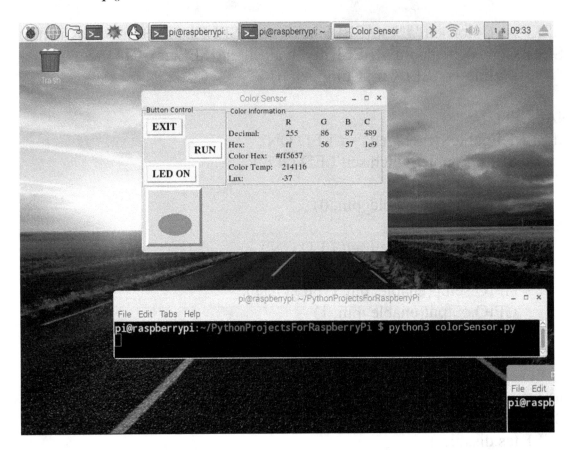

DC Motors Robot

You will need a robot chassis. I usually make mine from wood. Also a method to attach motors to the chassis. This is a simple robot that you can control from a Tkinter window. Consider a battery pack for the Raspberry, check specs carefully, there are many choices. I have setup the motors to run from the Raspberry 5V pin. Depending on your motor selection you many want to consider an additional power source for the motors, via the H-Bridge. The wiring diagram shows the motor power supply from the Raspberry and optional information if using a battery pack. As you increase voltage the chances of damaging your Raspberry increase. It can also help to add a capacitor to the breadboard to help with power surges when motors start.

I generally run my Raspberry "Headless". Currently using VNC Viewer. There are other options. Search for "Raspberry Headless". A starting point is
https://www.raspberrypi.org/documentation/remote-access/vnc/

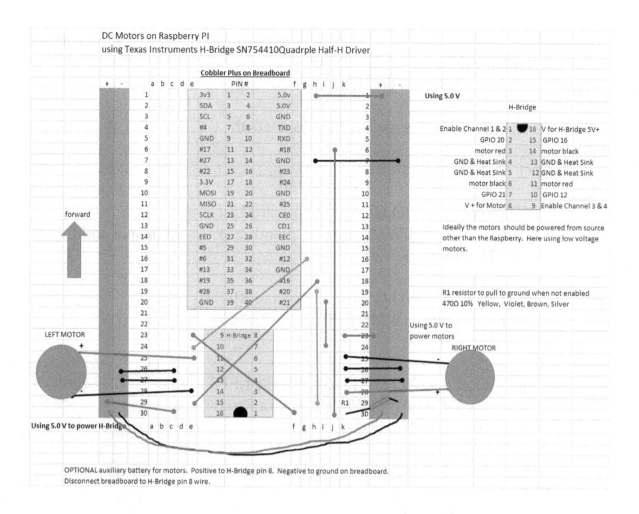

DC Motors on Raspberry PI
using Texas Instruments H-Bridge SN754410Quadrple Half-H Driver

```
# DC motor control with H-Bridge                    python3 DCMotorPyton3.py
# When running from cmd line make sure you use EXIT button to
# ensure that motors ports turn off
# RASPBERRY 3, python 3.4.2
# Herb Norbom, RyMax,Inc. 2/14/2017

from tkinter import *
#not using ttk as button repeatinterval not supported
#from tkinter.ttk import *
import tkinter.messagebox
from time import sleep
import RPi.GPIO as GPIO
GPIO.setmode(GPIO.BCM)
import sys
import signal
def signal_handler(signal, frame):          # SO CTRL + C  CAN STOP PROGRAM
    print("signal exit, run stopALL")       # if needed from command line
```

```python
        stopALL()                                #then position mouse over tkinter window
signal.signal(signal.SIGINT, signal_handler)
class SELF:                # set up, define later as needed
        pass
class self:                # set up, define later as needed
        pass
def motorSetup():
        try:
                GPIO.setup(21, GPIO.OUT)    # forward LEFT
                SELF.p21 = GPIO.PWM(21,SELF.pwmFreq)        # channel and frequency
                SELF.p21.start(100)

                GPIO.setup(16, GPIO.OUT)    # reverse RIGHT
                SELF.p16 = GPIO.PWM(16, SELF.pwmFreq)
                SELF.p16.start(100)

                GPIO.setup(20, GPIO.OUT)    # reverse LEFT
                SELF.p20 = GPIO.PWM(20, SELF.pwmFreq)
                SELF.p20.start(100)

                GPIO.setup(12, GPIO.OUT)    # forward RIGHT
                SELF.p12 = GPIO.PWM(12, SELF.pwmFreq)
                SELF.p12.start(100)
        except:
                print("error motor setup")
                print(sys.exc_info())

def BOTHREV():
        SELF.p21.start(SELF.dc)
        SELF.p12.start(SELF.dc)
        sleep(.2)
        SELF.p21.start(100)
        SELF.p12.start(100)

def revLeft():
        SELF.p21.start(SELF.dc)
        sleep(.2)
        SELF.p21.start(100)

def revRight():
```

```
        SELF.p12.start(SELF.dc)
        sleep(.2)
        SELF.p12.start(100)

def BOTHFWD():
        SELF.p20.start(SELF.dc)
        SELF.p16.start(SELF.dc)
        sleep(.2)
        SELF.p20.start(100)
        SELF.p16.start(100)

def fwdLeft():
        SELF.p20.start(SELF.dc)
        sleep(.2)
        SELF.p20.start(100)

def fwdRight():
        SELF.p16.start(SELF.dc )
        sleep(.1)
        SELF.p16.start(100)

def Setup():
        bF=LabelFrame(root,text="Button Control",width=90,height=90)
        bF.grid(column=0,row=0,stick=W)
        Button(bF, text='EXIT',command=stopALL).grid(column=0,row=0,sticky=W)

        SELF.EnableSwitch = StringVar()
        SELF.EnableSwitch.set('DISABLE H-Bridge')
        Button(bF, textvariable=SELF.EnableSwitch,
                command=ENABLE).grid(column=0,columnspan=3,row=4,sticky=W)
        Button(bF, text="Forward Left Motor",repeatdelay=50,repeatinterval=100,
                command=fwdLeft).grid(column=1,row=0,sticky=(W))
        Button(bF, text="Forward Right Motor",repeatdelay=50,repeatinterval=100,
                command=fwdRight).grid(column=2,row=0,sticky=(W))
        Button(bF, text="Reverse Left Motor",repeatdelay=50,repeatinterval=100,
                command=revLeft).grid(column=1,row=1,sticky=(W))
        Button(bF, text="Reverse Right Motor",repeatdelay=50,repeatinterval=100,
                command=revRight).grid(column=2,row=1,sticky=(W))
        Button(bF, text="BOTH Reverse",repeatdelay=50,repeatinterval=100,
                command=BOTHREV).grid(column=2,row=2,sticky=(W))
```

```
        Button(bF, text="BOTH Forward",repeatdelay=50,repeatinterval=100,
             command=BOTHFWD).grid(column=1,row=2,sticky=(W))
        Label(bF,text="HOLD BUTTON DOWN TO REPEAT",
             width=30).grid(column=0,columnspan=3,row=3)
        msg = "power level set at: " + str(SELF.dc)
        SELF.dcCurrent = StringVar()
        SELF.dcCurrent.set(str(msg))

        Label(bF,textvariable=SELF.dcCurrent, width=20).grid(column=0,
             columnspan=2,row=6)

        Label(bF,text= "Motor Power 0.0 - 100.0:").grid(column=0,columnspan=2,
             row=5,sticky=E)
        self.dc=Entry(bF, width=6)
        self.dc.insert(0, SELF.dc)
        self.dc.bind("<Return>", validate)
        self.dc.bind("<KP_Enter>", validate)
        self.dc.bind("<Tab>", validate)
        self.dc.grid(column=2,row=5,sticky =W)
        self.dc.focus()

def validate(event):
    try:
            SELF.dc=float(self.dc.get())
    except:
            tkinter.messagebox.showwarning("Power","Enter as \
                Integer or Decimal for motor power level.")
            self.dc.focus()
            return
    if SELF.dc < 0.0 or SELF.dc > 100.0:
            msg="Out of Range \n0.0 for maximum \nand \n100.0 for minimum."
            tkinter.messagebox.showwarning("Power",msg)
            self.dc.focus()
            return
    msg = "power level set at: " + str(SELF.dc)
    SELF.dcCurrent.set(msg)

def ENABLE():
    if SELF.EnableSwitch.get() =='ENABLE H-Bridge':
            SELF.EnableSwitch.set('DISABLE H-Bridge')
```

```
            enable_pin = 18
            GPIO.output(enable_pin, 0)
    else:
            SELF.EnableSwitch.set('ENABLE H-Bridge')
            enable_pin = 18
            GPIO.setup(enable_pin, GPIO.OUT)
            GPIO.output(enable_pin, 1)

def stopALL():
    print("stopALL called")
    GPIO.cleanup()          #need to run to reset all ports to off
    sleep(.1)
    root.destroy()

if __name__=="__main__":
    root=Tk()
    SELF.dc=20.5# Duty cycle % of time between pulses that signal on/off
                # range is 0.0 to 100.0, 100 is the lowest power setting
    SELF.pwmFreq=100      #Hz, number of times per second pulse generated
    root.title("Motor Controls")
    root.geometry("400x400+90+90")#width, height,x  and y placement
    motorSetup()
    Setup()
    mainloop()
```

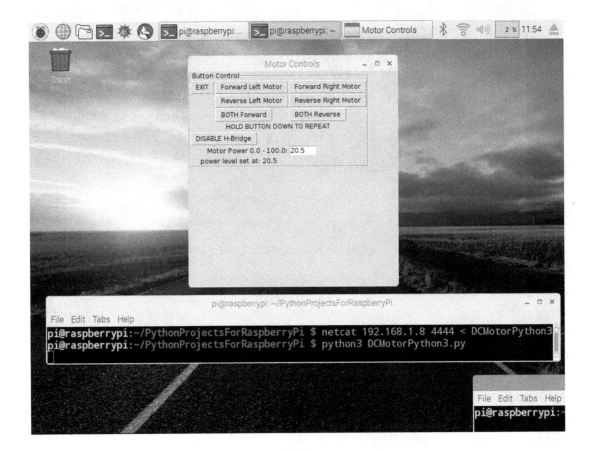

Robot Follow Black Tape

With this program we build on two of our previous programs. Our robot will be limited in what it can do, but I expect you will add features. This program will enable the robot to follow a black line (I used black electrical tape). The robot will go in a clockwise direction and only turn to the right. Start the robot on the black tape. To have the robot follow the tape in both directions you really need two sensors. At that point starting to get expensive. I would use two or more infrared detectors.

For some reason on my robot the left motor runs faster than the right motor. While running your robot try to get it to go straight by adjusting the motor duty cycles.

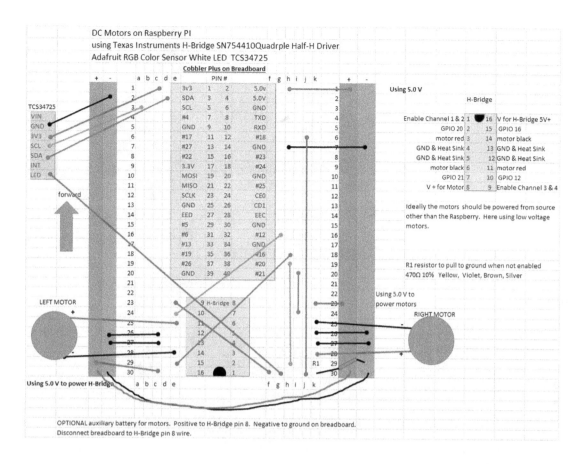

DC Motors on Raspberry PI
using Texas Instruments H-Bridge SN754410Quadrple Half-H Driver
Adafruit RGB Color Sensor White LED TCS34725

DC motor control with H-Bridge   python3 followBlackTapePython3.py
When running from cmd line make sure you use EXIT button to
ensure that motors ports turn off
RASPBERRY 3, python 3.4.2
Herb Norbom, RyMax,Inc. 2/16/2017
put robot on black tape path, will turn right only, run clockwise

```python
from tkinter import *
import tkinter.messagebox

from time import sleep
import RPi.GPIO as GPIO
GPIO.setmode(GPIO.BCM)
import threading
from threading import Thread
import sys
import signal
def signal_handler(signal, frame):          # SO CTRL + C  CAN STOP PROGRAM
    print("signal exit, run stopALL")       # if needed from command line
    stopALL()                               #then position mouse over tkinter window
```

```python
signal.signal(signal.SIGINT, signal_handler)

# Import the TCS34725 module.
import Adafruit_TCS34725
import smbus

class SELF:                  # set up, define later as needed
    pass
SELF.tcs = Adafruit_TCS34725.TCS34725()

class self:                  # set up, define later as needed
    pass
def motorSetup():
    try:
        GPIO.setup(21, GPIO.OUT)    # forward LEFT
        SELF.p21 = GPIO.PWM(21,SELF.pwmFreq)        # channel and frequency
        SELF.p21.start(100)

        GPIO.setup(16, GPIO.OUT)    # reverse RIGHT
        SELF.p16 = GPIO.PWM(16, SELF.pwmFreq)
        SELF.p16.start(100)

        GPIO.setup(20, GPIO.OUT)    # reverse LEFT
        SELF.p20 = GPIO.PWM(20, SELF.pwmFreq)
        SELF.p20.start(100)

        GPIO.setup(12, GPIO.OUT)    # forward RIGHT
        SELF.p12 = GPIO.PWM(12, SELF.pwmFreq)
        SELF.p12.start(100)
    except:
        print("error motor setup")
        print(sys.exc_info())

def BOTHREV():
    SELF.p21.start(SELF.leftDC)
    SELF.p12.start(SELF.rightDC)
    sleep(.1)
    SELF.p21.start(100)
    SELF.p12.start(100)
```

```
def fwdLeft():
    SELF.p21.start(SELF.leftDC)
    sleep(.1)
    SELF.p21.start(100)

def fwdRight():
    SELF.p12.start(SELF.rightDC)
    sleep(.1)
    SELF.p12.start(100)

def BOTHFWD():
    SELF.p20.start(SELF.leftDC)
    SELF.p16.start(SELF.rightDC)
    sleep(.1)
    SELF.p20.start(100)
    SELF.p16.start(100)

def revLeft():
    SELF.p20.start(SELF.leftDC)
    sleep(.1)
    SELF.p20.start(100)

def revRight():
    SELF.p16.start(SELF.rightDC )
    sleep(.1)
    SELF.p16.start(100)

def Setup():
    bF=LabelFrame(root,text="Button Control",width=90,height=90)
    bF.grid(column=0,row=0,stick=W)
    Button(bF,text='EXIT',command=stopALL,anchor=W).grid(column=0,row=0)
    SELF.dispSwitch = StringVar()
    SELF.dispSwitch.set('STOP')
    Button(bF, textvariable=SELF.dispSwitch,anchor=W,
            command=startRun).grid(column=1,columnspan=3,row=0)
    msg = "Right Motor set at: " + str(SELF.rightDC)
    SELF.rightDCCurrent = StringVar()
    SELF.rightDCCurrent.set(str(msg))

    Label(bF,textvariable=SELF.rightDCCurrent, width=20).grid(column=0,
```

```
                    columnspan=2,row=6)
        msg = "Left Motor set at: " + str(SELF.leftDC)
        SELF.leftDCCurrent = StringVar()
        SELF.leftDCCurrent.set(str(msg))

        Label(bF,textvariable=SELF.leftDCCurrent, width=20).grid(column=0,
                    columnspan=2,row=7)

        Label(bF,text= "Motor Power 0.0 - 100.0:",anchor = E).grid(column=0,
                    columnspan=2,row=2)
        Label(bF,text= "LEFT Motor",anchor = E).grid(column=0, row=3)
        Label(bF,text= "RIGHT Motor",anchor = E).grid(column=1,row=3)

        self.leftDC=Entry(bF, width=6)
        self.leftDC.insert(0, SELF.leftDC)
        self.leftDC.bind("<Return>", validateL)
        self.leftDC.bind("<KP_Enter>", validateL)
        self.leftDC.bind("<Tab>", validateL)
        self.leftDC.grid(column=0,row=5,sticky =W)
        self.leftDC.focus()

        self.rightDC=Entry(bF, width=6)
        self.rightDC.insert(0, SELF.rightDC)
        self.rightDC.bind("<Return>", validateR)
        self.rightDC.bind("<KP_Enter>", validateR)
        self.rightDC.bind("<Tab>", validateR)
        self.rightDC.grid(column=1,row=5,sticky =W)
        self.rightDC.focus()

        SELF.Canvas=Canvas(root, width =100, height=100, borderwidth=5,
                    relief=RAISED)
        SELF.Canvas.grid(column=0,row=2)

def startRun():
        if SELF.dispSwitch.get() == "RUN":
                SELF.dispSwitch.set("STOP")
                enable_pin = 18
                GPIO.output(enable_pin, 0)
        else:
                SELF.dispSwitch.set("RUN")
```

```python
            enable_pin = 18
            GPIO.setup(enable_pin, GPIO.OUT)
            GPIO.output(enable_pin, 1)

def validateR(event):
    try:
            SELF.rightDC=float(self.rightDC.get())
    except:
            tkinter.messagebox.showwarning("Power","Enter as \
                Integer or Decimal for motor power level.")
            self.rightDC.focus()
            return
    if SELF.rightDC < 0.0 or SELF.rightDC > 100.0:
            msg="Out of Range 0.0 for maximum and 100.0 for minimum."
            tkinter.messagebox.showwarning("Power",msg)
            self.rightDC.focus()
            return
    msg = "power level set at: " + str(SELF.rightDC)
    SELF.rightDCCurrent.set(msg)

def validateL(event):
    try:
            SELF.leftDC=float(self.leftDC.get())
    except:
            tkinter.messagebox.showwarning("Power","Enter as \
                Integer or Decimal for motor power level.")
            self.leftDC.focus()
            return
    if SELF.leftDC < 0.0 or SELF.leftDC > 100.0:
            msg="Out of Range 0.0 for maximum and 100.0 for minimum."
            tkinter.messagebox.showwarning("Power",msg)
            self.leftDC.focus()
            return
    msg = "power level set at: " + str(SELF.leftDC)
    SELF.leftDCCurrent.set(msg)

def displayUPDATING():
    SELF.coloR = 17                  #arbitrary starting values
    SELF.coloG = 12
    SELF.coloB = 36
```

```python
        SELF.coloC = 100
        SELF.color_temp =1000
        SELF.lux = 500
        SELF.dDir = "Direction: STRAIGHT"

        SELF.dF=LabelFrame(root,text="Color Information",width=90,height=90)
        SELF.dF.grid(column=1,columnspan=3,row=0,stick=W)
        Label(SELF.dF,text="R ",width=4).grid(column=1,row=0)
        Label(SELF.dF,text="G ",width=4).grid(column=2,row=0)
        Label(SELF.dF,text="B ",width=4).grid(column=3,row=0)
        Label(SELF.dF,text="C ",width=4).grid(column=4,row=0)
#decimal values
        Label(SELF.dF,text="Decimal:",width=11).grid(column=0,row=1)
        SELF.dR = StringVar()
        SELF.dR.set(str(SELF.coloR))
        L1=Label(SELF.dF,textvariable=SELF.dR, width=4)
        L1.grid(column=1,row=1)

        SELF.dG = StringVar()
        SELF.dG.set(str(SELF.coloG))
        Label(SELF.dF,textvariable=SELF.dG, width=4).grid(column=2,row=1)

        SELF.dB = StringVar()
        SELF.dB.set(str(SELF.coloB))
        Label(SELF.dF,textvariable=SELF.dB, width=4).grid(column=3,row=1)

        SELF.dC = StringVar()
        SELF.dC.set(str(SELF.coloC))
        Label(SELF.dF,textvariable=SELF.dC, width=4).grid(column=4,row=1)

#hex values
        Label(SELF.dF,text="Hex:",width=11).grid(column=0,row=2)
        SELF.hexR = '{0:02x}'.format(SELF.coloR)
        SELF.hexG = '{0:02x}'.format(SELF.coloG)
        SELF.hexB = '{0:02x}'.format(SELF.coloB)
        SELF.hexC = '{0:02x}'.format(SELF.coloC)

        SELF.hR = StringVar()
        SELF.hR.set(str(SELF.hexR))
        Label(SELF.dF,textvariable=SELF.hR, width=4).grid(column=1,row=2)
```

```python
SELF.hG = StringVar()
SELF.hG.set(str(SELF.hexG))
Label(SELF.dF,textvariable=SELF.hG, width=4).grid(column=2,row=2)

SELF.hB = StringVar()
SELF.hB.set(str(SELF.hexB))
Label(SELF.dF,textvariable=SELF.hB, width=4).grid(column=3,row=2)

SELF.hC = StringVar()
SELF.hC.set(str(SELF.hexC))
Label(SELF.dF,textvariable=SELF.hC, width=4).grid(column=4,row=2)

Label(SELF.dF,text="Color Hex:",width=11).grid(column=0,row=3)
myColor="#"+str(SELF.hexR)+str(SELF.hexG)+str(SELF.hexB)
SELF.myColor= StringVar()
SELF.myColor.set("#"+str(SELF.hexR)+str(SELF.hexG)+str(SELF.hexB))
Label(SELF.dF,textvariable=SELF.myColor, width=16,
      anchor=W).grid(column=1,columnspan=2,row=3)

Label(SELF.dF,text="Color Temp:",width=11).grid(column=0,row=4)
SELF.dColorTemp = StringVar()
SELF.dColorTemp.set(str(SELF.color_temp))
Label(SELF.dF,textvariable=SELF.dColorTemp,
      width=6).grid(column=1,row=4)

Label(SELF.dF,text="Lux:",width=11).grid(column=0,row=5)
SELF.dLux = StringVar()
SELF.dLux.set(str(SELF.lux))
Label(SELF.dF,textvariable=SELF.dLux, width=6).grid(column=1,row=5)

SELF.ddDir = StringVar()
SELF.ddDir.set(str(SELF.dDir))
Label(root,textvariable=SELF.ddDir, width=23,
      anchor=W).grid(column=1,row=2)

SELF.myOval=SELF.Canvas.create_oval(25,50,90,90,fill=myColor,
      outline=myColor)

while True:  #running via thread so can have control to stop
```

```python
        if SELF.dispSwitch.get()=="RUN":
            try:
                # Read the R, G, B, C color data.
                SELF.coloR, SELF.coloG, SELF.coloB, \
                    SELF.coloC = SELF.tcs.get_raw_data()
                # Calculate color temperature using utility functions.
#the following 3 lines are one line of code, not able to format well in printed version
                SELF.color_temp = \
Adafruit_TCS34725.calculate_color_temperature(SELF.coloR, \
                    SELF.coloG, SELF.coloB)

                # Calculate lux with another utility function.
                SELF.lux = Adafruit_TCS34725.calculate_lux(SELF.coloR,
                    SELF.coloG, SELF.coloB)

                updateColors()
                if SELF.coloR < 90:        #adjust as needed
                    BOTHFWD()
                    SELF.dDir = "Direction: STRAIGHT"
                else:
                    revLeft()
                    SELF.dDir = "Direction: RIGHT"
                sleep(.3)
                SELF.lastcoloR = SELF.coloR
            except:
                print("Error on Color Sensor")

def updateColors():
    if SELF.coloR > 255:
        SELF.coloR = 255
    if SELF.coloG > 255:
        SELF.coloG = 255
    if SELF.coloB > 255:
        SELF.coloB = 255
    SELF.dR.set(SELF.coloR)
    SELF.dG.set(SELF.coloG)
    SELF.dB.set(SELF.coloB)
    SELF.dC.set(SELF.coloC)
    SELF.hexR = '{0:02x}'.format(SELF.coloR)
    SELF.hexG = '{0:02x}'.format(SELF.coloG)
```

```python
        SELF.hexB = '{0:02x}'.format(SELF.coloB)
        SELF.hexC = '{0:02x}'.format(SELF.coloC)
        SELF.hR.set(str(SELF.hexR))
        SELF.hG.set(str(SELF.hexG))
        SELF.hB.set(str(SELF.hexB))
        SELF.hC.set(str(SELF.hexC))

        SELF.dColorTemp.set(str(SELF.color_temp))
        SELF.dLux.set(str(SELF.lux))

        SELF.myColor.set("#"+str(SELF.hexR)+str(SELF.hexG)+str(SELF.hexB))
        SELF.Canvas.itemconfig(SELF.myOval,fill=str(SELF.myColor.get()), \
            outline=str(SELF.myColor.get()))
        try:
            SELF.ddDir.set(str(SELF.dDir))
        except:
            print("ERROR 298")

def stopALL():
        print("stopALL called")
        GPIO.cleanup()              #need to run to reset all ports
        SELF.tcs.set_interrupt(True)
        SELF.tcs.disable()
        sleep(.1)
        root.destroy()

def threadStart():
        dispTh=Thread(target=displayUPDATING, name='dispMSG',args=())
        dispTh.setDaemon(True)
        try:
            dispTh.start()
        except:
            print(sys.exc_info())

if __name__=="__main__":
        root=Tk()
        SELF.rightDC=2.5# Duty cycle % of time between pulses that signal
            # on/off range is 0.0 to 100.0, 100 is the lowest power setting
        SELF.leftDC=28.5
        SELF.pwmFreq=100        #Hz,number of times per second pulse generated
```

```
root.title("Follow Black Tape Controls")
root.geometry("525x275+90+90")#width, height,x  and y placement
motorSetup()
Setup()
threadStart()
mainloop()
```

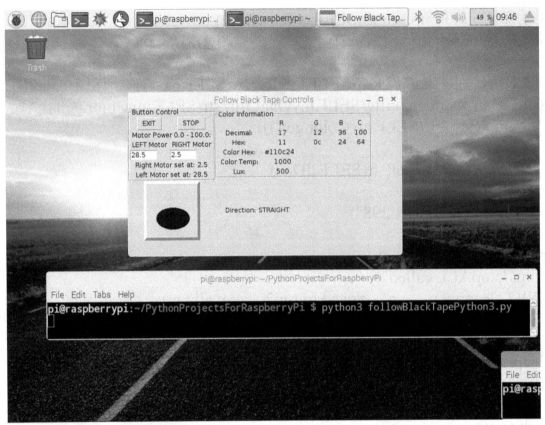

DC Motors Infrared Detectors

This will build a black tape line follower that can turn left and right and truly follow the track. You will need two infrared LED/Sensors. Mount them approximately 1 ½ inches apart on the front of your robot. They should be approximately 1/8 to 1/4 inch off the ground. They work best with a light shield around them. This project also uses the Adafruit ADS1015 12-Bit ADC to convert the infrared sensor signal to digital.

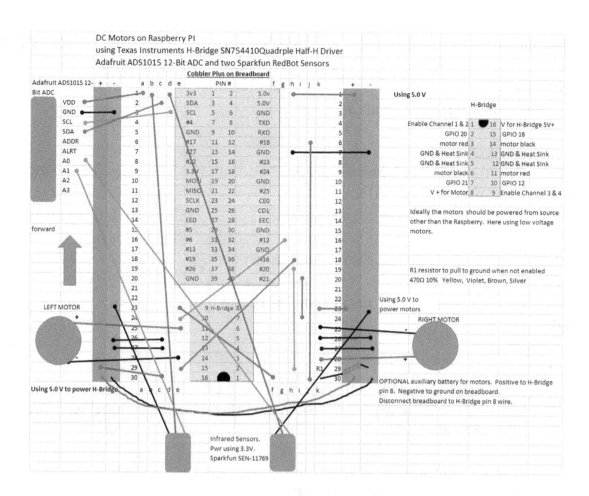

DC Motors on Raspberry PI
using Texas Instruments H-Bridge SN754410Quadrple Half-H Driver
Adafruit ADS1015 12-Bit ADC and two Sparkfun RedBot Sensors

python3 followBlackInfraredPython3.py
DC motors, H-Bridge, two infrared detectors
When running from cmd line make sure you use EXIT button to
ensure that motors ports turn off
RASPBERRY 3, python 3.4.2
Herb Norbom, RyMax,Inc. 2/17/2017
robot will go straight until it finds black tape path

```python
from tkinter import *
import tkinter.messagebox

from time import sleep
import RPi.GPIO as GPIO
GPIO.setmode(GPIO.BCM)
import threading
from threading import Thread
import sys
import signal
```

```python
def signal_handler(signal, frame):              # SO CTRL + C  CAN STOP PROGRAM
        print("signal exit, run stopALL")       # if needed from command line
        stopALL()                               #then position mouse over tkinter window
signal.signal(signal.SIGINT, signal_handler)

import Adafruit_ADS1x15
# Create an ADS1015 ADC (12-bit) instance.
adc = Adafruit_ADS1x15.ADS1015()
GAIN = 1

class SELF:                 # set up, define later as needed
        pass
class self:                 # set up, define later as needed
        pass
def motorSetup():
        try:
                GPIO.setup(21, GPIO.OUT)     # forward LEFT
                SELF.p21 = GPIO.PWM(21,SELF.pwmFreq)          # channel and frequency
                SELF.p21.start(100)

                GPIO.setup(16, GPIO.OUT)     # reverse RIGHT
                SELF.p16 = GPIO.PWM(16, SELF.pwmFreq)
                SELF.p16.start(100)

                GPIO.setup(20, GPIO.OUT)     # reverse LEFT
                SELF.p20 = GPIO.PWM(20, SELF.pwmFreq)
                SELF.p20.start(100)

                GPIO.setup(12, GPIO.OUT)     # forward RIGHT
                SELF.p12 = GPIO.PWM(12, SELF.pwmFreq)
                SELF.p12.start(100)
        except:
                print("error motor setup")
                print(sys.exc_info())

def BOTHREV():
        SELF.p21.start(SELF.leftDC)
        SELF.p12.start(SELF.rightDC)
        sleep(.1)
        SELF.p21.start(100)
```

```python
        SELF.p12.start(100)

def fwdLeft():
        SELF.p20.start(SELF.leftDC)
        sleep(.1)
        SELF.p20.start(100)

def fwdRight():
        SELF.p16.start(SELF.rightDC)
        sleep(.1)
        SELF.p16.start(100)

def BOTHFWD():
        SELF.p20.start(SELF.leftDC)
        SELF.p16.start(SELF.rightDC)
        sleep(.1)
        SELF.p20.start(100)
        SELF.p16.start(100)

def revLeft():
        SELF.p21.start(SELF.leftDC)
        sleep(.1)
        SELF.p21.start(100)

def revRight():
        SELF.p12.start(SELF.rightDC )
        sleep(.05)
        SELF.p12.start(100)

def Setup():
        bF=LabelFrame(root,text="Button Control",width=90,height=90)
        bF.grid(column=0,row=0,stick=W)
        Button(bF,text='EXIT',command=stopALL,anchor=W).grid(column=0,row=0)
        SELF.dispSwitch = StringVar()
        SELF.dispSwitch.set('STOP')
        Button(bF, textvariable=SELF.dispSwitch,anchor=W,
                command=startRun).grid(column=1,columnspan=3,row=0)
        msg = "Right Motor set at: " + str(SELF.rightDC)
        SELF.rightDCCurrent = StringVar()
        SELF.rightDCCurrent.set(str(msg))
```

```python
Label(bF,textvariable=SELF.rightDCCurrent, width=20).grid(column=0,
        columnspan=2,row=6)
msg = "Left Motor set at: " + str(SELF.leftDC)
SELF.leftDCCurrent = StringVar()
SELF.leftDCCurrent.set(str(msg))

Label(bF,textvariable=SELF.leftDCCurrent, width=20).grid(column=0,
        columnspan=2,row=7)

Label(bF,text= "Motor Power 0.0 - 100.0:",anchor = E).grid(column=0,
        columnspan=2,row=2)
Label(bF,text= "LEFT Motor",anchor = E).grid(column=0, row=3)
Label(bF,text= "RIGHT Motor",anchor = E).grid(column=1,row=3)

self.leftDC=Entry(bF, width=6)
self.leftDC.insert(0, SELF.leftDC)
self.leftDC.bind("<Return>", validateL)
self.leftDC.bind("<KP_Enter>", validateL)
self.leftDC.bind("<Tab>", validateL)
self.leftDC.grid(column=0,row=5,sticky =W)
self.leftDC.focus()

self.rightDC=Entry(bF, width=6)
self.rightDC.insert(0, SELF.rightDC)
self.rightDC.bind("<Return>", validateR)
self.rightDC.bind("<KP_Enter>", validateR)
self.rightDC.bind("<Tab>", validateR)
self.rightDC.grid(column=1,row=5,sticky =W)
self.rightDC.focus()

def startRun():
    if SELF.dispSwitch.get() == "RUN":
        SELF.dispSwitch.set("STOP")
        enable_pin = 18
        GPIO.output(enable_pin, 0)
    else:
        SELF.dispSwitch.set("RUN")
        enable_pin = 18
        GPIO.setup(enable_pin, GPIO.OUT)
```

```python
            GPIO.output(enable_pin, 1)

    def validateR(event):
        try:
                SELF.rightDC=float(self.rightDC.get())
        except:
                tkinter.messagebox.showwarning("Power","Enter as \
                    Integer or Decimal for motor power level.")
                self.rightDC.focus()
                return
        if SELF.rightDC < 0.0 or SELF.rightDC > 100.0:
                msg="Out of Range 0.0 for maximum and 100.0 for minimum."
                tkinter.messagebox.showwarning("Power",msg)
                self.rightDC.focus()
                return
        msg = "power level set at: " + str(SELF.rightDC)
        SELF.rightDCCurrent.set(msg)

    def validateL(event):
        try:
                SELF.leftDC=float(self.leftDC.get())
        except:
                tkinter.messagebox.showwarning("Power","Enter as \
                    Integer or Decimal for motor power level.")
                self.leftDC.focus()
                return
        if SELF.leftDC < 0.0 or SELF.leftDC > 100.0:
                msg="Out of Range 0.0 for maximum and 100.0 for minimum."
                tkinter.messagebox.showwarning("Power",msg)
                self.leftDC.focus()
                return
        msg = "power level set at: " + str(SELF.leftDC)
        SELF.leftDCCurrent.set(msg)

def displayUPDATING():
    SELF.infraredLeft = 1000                     #arbitrary starting values
    SELF.infraredRight= 1000
    SELF.dDir = "Direction: STRAIGHT"
    SELF.dF=LabelFrame(root,text="Infrared Detector",width=25,height=90)
    SELF.dF.grid(column=1,columnspan=3,row=0,stick=W)
```

```
        Label(SELF.dF,text="LEFT ",width=6).grid(column=1,row=0)
        Label(SELF.dF,text="RIGHT ",width=6).grid(column=2,row=0)

#infrared values
        SELF.dL = StringVar()
        SELF.dL.set(str(SELF.infraredLeft))
        Label(SELF.dF,textvariable=SELF.dL, width=6).grid(column=1,row=1)

        SELF.dR = StringVar()
        SELF.dR.set(str(SELF.infraredRight))
        Label(SELF.dF,textvariable=SELF.dR, width=6).grid(column=2,row=1)

        SELF.ddDir = StringVar()
        SELF.ddDir.set(str(SELF.dDir))
        Label(root,textvariable=SELF.ddDir, width=23,
                anchor=W).grid(column=1,row=2)


        while True:  #running via thread so can have control to stop
                if SELF.dispSwitch.get()=="RUN":
# Read the two ADC channel values into a list.
                        values = [0]*2       # define a list of two with zero value
                        try:
                                for i in range(2):
                                        values[i] = adc.read_adc(i, gain=GAIN)
                        except:
#                                print(sys.exc_info())
                                pass #occansional errors, not sure if poor soldering or
                                        # something in wiring, if too severe you need to find
                                        # cause
                        SELF.infraredLeft=str('{:0}'.format(values[0]))
                        SELF.infraredRight=str('{:0}'.format(values[1]))
                        sleep(0.2)
                        tempR = int(SELF.infraredRight)
                        tempL = int(SELF.infraredLeft)
                        if tempR < 900 and tempL < 900:                    #adjust as needed
                                BOTHFWD()
                                SELF.dDir = "Direction: STRAIGHT"
                        elif tempR >= 900:
                                revLeft()
                                fwdRight()
```

```python
                SELF.dDir = "Direction: LEFT"
            else:

                SELF.dDir = "Direction: RIGHT"
                revRight()
                fwdLeft()
            updateDisplay()

def updateDisplay():
    SELF.dR.set(SELF.infraredRight)
    SELF.dL.set(SELF.infraredLeft)
    try:
            SELF.ddDir.set(str(SELF.dDir))
    except:
            pass

def stopALL():
    print("stopALL called")
    SELF.dispSwitch.set("STOP")
    sleep(.2)
    GPIO.cleanup()              #need to run to reset all ports
    sleep(.1)
    root.destroy()

def threadStart():
    dispTh=Thread(target=displayUPDATING, name='dispMSG',args=())
    dispTh.setDaemon(True)
    try:
            dispTh.start()
    except:
            print(sys.exc_info())

if __name__=="__main__":
    root=Tk()
    SELF.rightDC=2.5# Duty cycle % of time between pulses that signal
            # on/off range is 0.0 to 100.0, 100 is the lowest power setting
            # my right motor needs more power, adjust left and right to
            # get robot moving in straight line
    SELF.leftDC=28.5
    SELF.pwmFreq=100        #Hz,number of times per second pulse generated
    root.title("Infrared Detector")
```

```
root.geometry("325x180+90+90")#width, height,x  and y placement
motorSetup()
Setup()
threadStart()
mainloop()
```

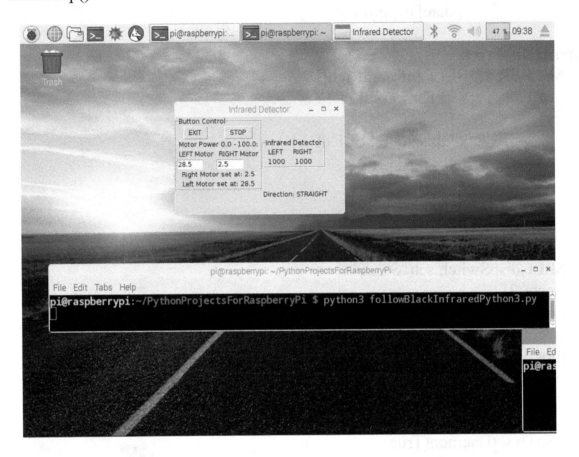

Balance Bot

There are several programs included with the book and more available for a limited time in the software purchase. The goal of this section is to give you the tools to read the MPU6050 and achieve self balancing.

There are many variables to consider. In building your bot consider the height, width and weight. Ideally your bot should come close to balancing without any power being supplied. In general a taller bot is easier to balance. The weight placed higher is generally better. All within reason. I tried many configurations of bots in height, weight, motor type and power supply. Even using the smaller motors used in other projects you may find the need for an external power supply for the motors. I am using a 9.6 V battery pack. You need geared motors, the ones we have been using in other projects do work. If you go for more powerful motors the need for an external power supply will be required.

Your bot will fall over many times while you are getting the settings correct. Plan on having a hand on it or a protection bar of some sort. Protect the Raspberry. I am not sure if I have some sort of problem with the hardware, but the calibration needs to be run at least every day as the readings change to some degree. I also find that the Rotation value adjustment needs to be used more frequently than I expected. The program provides for you to run the MPU6050 and print some values to the console.

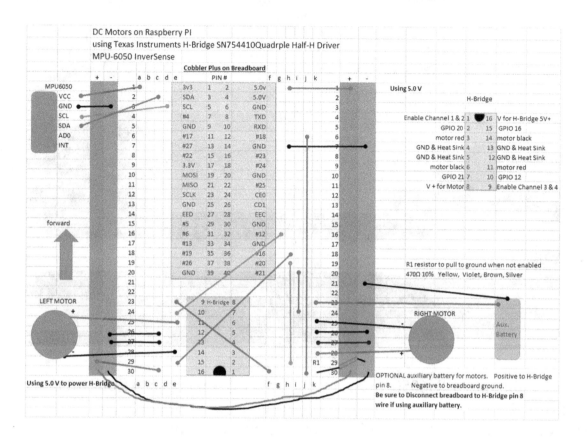

I have the MPU6050 mounted high in a directional manner that lets me use the Y axis as my main control. All the pins of the MPU6050 are facing forward.

MPU6050CALIBRATION

The first program I have listed is a simple MPU6050 calibration program. This program can also read the temperature and chip identifier. To calibrate set the bot on a level stable service and run the calibration program first. This will write the calibration factors to a file that is read by the balance bot program.

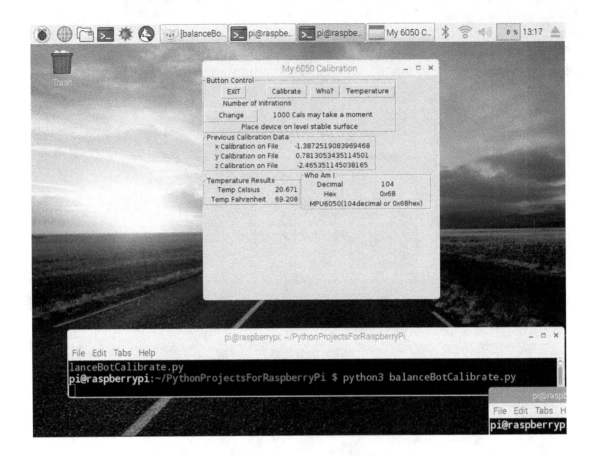

```
# python3 Calibrate MPU6050                python3 balanceBotCalibrate.py
# RASPBERRY 3
# Herb Norbom, RyMax,Inc. 2/20/2017 for personal use only

import smbus
import time
import math
import time
import sys                    #need as writing temp file
from time import sleep
from tkinter import *
import tkinter.messagebox

class SELF:
        pass              # set up, define later as needed

def setupDisplay():
        SELF.bFrame=LabelFrame(root,text="Button Control")
        SELF.bFrame.grid(column=0,columnspan=3,row=0,stick=W)
```

```python
        Button(SELF.bFrame, text='EXIT',
            command=root.destroy).grid(column=0,row=0)
        Button(SELF.bFrame, text='Calibrate',
            command=calibrate).grid(column=1,row=0)
        Button(SELF.bFrame, text='Who?',
            command=getWhoAmI).grid(column=2,row=0)
        Button(SELF.bFrame, text='Temperature',
            command=getTemperature).grid(column=3,row=0)
        Label(SELF.bFrame, text = "Number of Initrations",
            width=25).grid(column=0,columnspan=2,row =5,sticky=(N,E,S))
        Button(SELF.bFrame, text="Change",width = 10,
            command=nuCalibrations).grid(column=0, row=6, sticky=(N,W,S))
        msg = str(SELF.setCalNumber)+" Cals may take a moment"
        Label(SELF.bFrame,text=msg,width=28).grid(column=1,columnspan=3,
            row =6,sticky=(W))
        Label(SELF.bFrame,text="Place device on level stable surface",
            width=36).grid(column=0,columnspan=4,row =7)
        preCalibration()

def preCalibration():
        SELF.prevDataFrame=LabelFrame(root,text="Previous Calibration Data")
        SELF.prevDataFrame.grid(column=0,columnspan=3,row=1,stick=W)
        Label(SELF.prevDataFrame,text="x Calibration on File",
            width=20).grid(column =0, row =2)
        Label(SELF.prevDataFrame,text=SELF.xAdj,width=20).grid(column=1,row=2)

        Label(SELF.prevDataFrame,text="y Calibration on File",
            width=20).grid(column =0, row =3)
        Label(SELF.prevDataFrame,text=SELF.yAdj,width=20).grid(column =1,row=3)

        Label(SELF.prevDataFrame,text="z Calibration on File",
            width=20).grid(column =0, row =4)
        Label(SELF.prevDataFrame,text=SELF.zAdj,width=20).grid(column =1,row=4)

def nuCalibrations():
        SELF.temp=Entry(SELF.bFrame,width=10)
        SELF.temp.insert(0,SELF.setCalNumber)
        SELF.temp.grid(column=0,row=6)
        SELF.temp.bind("<Return>",myValidate)
        SELF.temp.bind("<KP_Enter>",myValidate)
```

```python
        SELF.temp.bind("<Tab>",myValidate)
        SELF.temp.focus()

def myValidate(event):
    try:
            test=int(SELF.temp.get())
            SELF.setCalNumber = test

            if SELF.setCalNumber < 1:
                tkinter.messagebox.showwarning('Warning',
                    'Value cannot be negative  or zero')
                SELF.setCalNumber=1000
                nuCalibrations()
    except:
            tkinter.messagebox.showwarning("Error",
                "Value must be an Integer")
            SELF.setCalNumber=1000
            nuCalibrations()
    msg = str(SELF.setCalNumber)+" Cals may take a moment"
    Label(SELF.bFrame,text=msg,width=28).grid(column=1,columnspan=3,
            row=6,sticky=(W))


def getTemperature():
    raw_temp = read_word(0x41)
    SELF.tempFrame=LabelFrame(root,text="Temperature Results",height=90)
    SELF.tempFrame.grid(column=0,row=2, sticky=W)
    Label(SELF.tempFrame,text="Temp Celsius",width=16).grid(column=0,row=0)
    temp=(raw_temp/340)+36.53
    Label(SELF.tempFrame,text="{:5.3f}".format(temp),
            width=6).grid(column =1, row =0)
    Label(SELF.tempFrame,text="Temp
Fahrenheit",width=16).grid(column=0,row=1)
    temp=temp*9/5+32.0
    Label(SELF.tempFrame,text="{:5.3f}".format(temp),
            width=6).grid(column =1, row =1)


def read_byte(adr):
    return SELF.bus.read_byte_data(SELF.address, adr)


def read_word(adr):
```

```python
        high = SELF.bus.read_byte_data(SELF.address, adr)
        low = SELF.bus.read_byte_data(SELF.address, adr+1)
        temp = (high <<8)
        val = (high << 8) + low
        if (val >= 32768):                      #decimal value 32,768, HEX 0x8000
                temp = -((65535 - val) + 1)
                return -((65535 - val) + 1)
        else:
                return val


def read_word_2c(adr):
        val = read_word(adr)
        if (val >= 32768):                      #decimal value 32,768, HEX 0x8000
                temp = -((65535 - val) + 1)
                return -((65535 - val) + 1)
        else:
                return val


def write_byte(adr, value):
        SELF.bus.write_byte_data(SELF.address, adr, value)


def readData():                 # read txt file see if prev data available
        try:
                with open('calData.txt','r') as f:
                        SELF.xAdj=float(f.readline())
                        SELF.yAdj=float(f.readline())
                        SELF.zAdj=float(f.readline())
        except:
                msg= "File calData.txt will be created in current Directory"
                tkinter.messagebox.showwarning("Warning",msg)
                SELF.xAdj = 0.0
                SELF.yAdj = 0.0
                SELF.zAdj = 0.0


def calibrate():
        SELF.calFrame=LabelFrame(root,text="Calibrate Results",
                width=50,height=90)
        SELF.calFrame.grid(column=0,columnspan=3,row=8)
        readData()                      # read previous calibration data stored in file
        preCalibration()
```

```python
        xout = 0
        yout = 0
        zout =0
        myCount =0
        while myCount < int(SELF.setCalNumber):
                xTemp = (read_word_2c(0x43)/SELF.gLSB)        # gyro x  out
                xout = xout + xTemp
                yTemp = read_word_2c(0x45)/SELF.gLSB          # gyro y  out
                yout = yout + yTemp
                zTemp = read_word_2c(0x47)/SELF.gLSB          # gyro z  out
                zout = zout + zTemp
                myCount = myCount + 1
                    #values from calibration program, sign flip in balanceBot
        xAdj = xout/int(SELF.setCalNumber)
        yAdj = yout/int(SELF.setCalNumber)
        zAdj = zout/int(SELF.setCalNumber)

        Label(SELF.calFrame,text="Counted",width=20).grid(column=0,row=0)
        Label(SELF.calFrame,text=myCount).grid(column =1, row =0)

        Label(SELF.calFrame,text="x Average",width=20).grid(column=0, row=2)
        Label(SELF.calFrame,text=xout/int(SELF.setCalNumber),
            width=20).grid(column =1, row =2)

        Label(SELF.calFrame,text="y Average",width=20).grid(column=0, row=3)
        Label(SELF.calFrame,text=yout/int(SELF.setCalNumber),
            width=20).grid(column =1, row =3)

        Label(SELF.calFrame,text="z Average",width=20).grid(column=0, row=4)
        Label(SELF.calFrame,text=zout/int(SELF.setCalNumber),
            width=20).grid(column =1, row =4)

        with open('calData.txt','w') as f:
                f.write(str(xAdj))
                f.write("\n")
                f.write(str(yAdj))
                f.write("\n")
                f.write(str(zAdj))


def stopALL():
```

```python
        SELF.TOP.destroy()

def getWhoAmI():
        who=read_byte(0x75)                    #should return 0x68 or indecimal 104
        SELF.whoFrame=LabelFrame(root,text="Who Am I ",width=50,height=90)
        SELF.whoFrame.grid(column=1,row=2)
        Label(SELF.whoFrame,text="Decimal",width=10).grid(column =0, row=0)
        Label(SELF.whoFrame,text=who,width=10).grid(column =1, row =0)
        Label(SELF.whoFrame,text="Hex",width=10).grid(column =0, row =1)
        Label(SELF.whoFrame,text=hex(who),width=10).grid(column =1, row =1)
        Label(SELF.whoFrame,text="MPU6050(104decimal or 0x68hex)",
                width=30).grid(column=0,columnspan=3,row=2,sticky=W)

def setupTk():
        SELF.setCalNumber = 1000
        readData()                    # read previous calibration data stored in file
        setupDisplay()
        # Power management registers and setup for MPU6050
        SELF.gLSB=131.0               #for gyroscope outputs reg 1B page 14   +-250
        SELF.aLSB=16384.0     #for accelerometer outputs reg 1C page 15       +-2g
        SELF.bus = smbus.SMBus(1) # for Revision 2 boards
        SELF.address = 0x68        # This is the address value i2c
        SELF.power_mgmt_1 = 0x6b   #the Hex converts to 107 as decimal
        SELF.power_mgmt_2 = 0x6c   #the Hex converts to 108 as decimal
        # Wake the 6050 up, it starts in sleep mode
        write_byte(SELF.power_mgmt_1, 0x00)     #Datasheet page 40,
                                                #clksel=internal 8Mhz
        sleep(1)                  #pause for wakeup

if __name__=="__main__":
        root= Tk()
        root.title("My 6050 Calibration")
        root.geometry("450x415+1+10")#width, height, x location, y location
        setupTk()
        mainloop()
```

Balance Bot

With the bot still on a level surface run balanceBotPython3.py with the motors off. Adjust the "last_y" value until the "temp" is hovering around 0.0. Run it several times.

While I could get the bot to achieve limited success in balancing, it is not perfect. There is oscillation and after a short period the bot does exceed the limits and falls over. I did use different motors in this project. I used Sparkfun ROB-13258, 65 RPM and a gear ratio of 48:1 vs. ROB-13302, 140 RPM and a gear ratio of 48:1.

```
#                                           python3 balanceBotPython3.py
# credit to following for assistance
# blog.bitify.co.uk/2013/11/reading-data-from-mpu-6050-on-raspberry.html
# python: 3.4.2 on Raspberry Pi
# MPU-6050 InvenSense reference MPU-6000/MPU6050 Register Map
# Herb Norbom 2/27/2017
import smbus
import math
import time
```

```python
from time import sleep
from tkinter import *
import threading
from threading import Thread
import RPi.GPIO as GPIO
GPIO.setmode(GPIO.BCM)

bus = smbus.SMBus(1)   # for Revision 2 boards
address = 0x68      # This is the address value for MPU6050

bus.write_byte_data(address, 0x6B, 0)# wake 6050 up,starts in sleep mode
sleep(.3)

class SELF:
        pass                # set up, define later as needed
SELF.run = True             #to keep loop in thread running

try:
        with open('calData.txt','r') as f:
                xAdj=float(f.readline())# values from calibrate6050.py program
                yAdj=float(f.readline())# which writes calData.txt
                zAdj=float(f.readline())# if file exists the file data is used
except:
        print("Warning! Calibration factors are zero.")
        sleep(3)                #pause to allow for time to read message
        xAdj = 0.0
        yAdj = 0.0
        zAdj = 0.0

gyro_scale = 131.0
accel_scale = 16384.0
def read_all():        # using block data start at address and read 6 bytes
                       # start with GYRO_XOUT and ends with GYRO_ZOUT page 31
        try:
                raw_gyro_data = bus.read_i2c_block_data(address, 0x43, 6)
                raw_accel_data = bus.read_i2c_block_data(address, 0x3b, 6)

                gyro_scaled_x = (breakWord((raw_gyro_data[0] << 8) + \
                        raw_gyro_data[1]) / gyro_scale) + xAdj
                gyro_scaled_y = (breakWord((raw_gyro_data[2] << 8) + \
```

```python
                    raw_gyro_data[3]) / gyro_scale) + yAdj
            gyro_scaled_z = (breakWord((raw_gyro_data[4] << 8) + \
                    raw_gyro_data[5]) / gyro_scale) + zAdj

            accel_scaled_x = breakWord((raw_accel_data[0] << 8) + \
                    raw_accel_data[1]) / accel_scale
            accel_scaled_y = breakWord((raw_accel_data[2] << 8) + \
                    raw_accel_data[3]) / accel_scale
            accel_scaled_z = breakWord((raw_accel_data[4] << 8) + \
                    raw_accel_data[5]) / accel_scale

            return (gyro_scaled_x, gyro_scaled_y, gyro_scaled_z,
                    accel_scaled_x, accel_scaled_y, accel_scaled_z)
        except:
            print("ERROR MPU6050 read")

def breakWord(word):
    if (word >= 0x8000):
            return -((65535 - word) + 1)
    else:
            return word

def dist(a,b):
    return math.sqrt((a * a) + (b * b))

def get_y_rotation(x,y,z):
    radians = math.atan2(x, dist(y,z))
    return -math.degrees(radians)

def get_x_rotation(x,y,z):
    radians = math.atan2(y, dist(x,z))
    return math.degrees(radians)

def run6050loop():
    try:                                        # in Frequency higher is faster
            GPIO.setup(21, GPIO.LOW)    # forward LEFT
            p21 = GPIO.PWM(21,100)              # channel and frequency
            p21.start(100)                      # effective off value
            GPIO.setup(16, GPIO.LOW)    # reverse RIGHT
            p16 = GPIO.PWM(16, 100)
```

```python
                p16.start(100)
                GPIO.setup(20, GPIO.LOW)    # reverse LEFT
                p20 = GPIO.PWM(20, 100)
                p20.start(100)
                GPIO.setup(12, GPIO.LOW)    # forward RIGHT
                p12 = GPIO.PWM(12, 100)
                p12.start(100)
        except:
                print("ERROR motor")

#set starting values for PID
        set_point = .0
        P = 1.1
        I = 0.001
        D = 0.001
        Integrator = 0.0
        Integrator_Max = 7.0
        Integrator_Min = -7.0


        fwdStart = .37            # setup range where motors will kick in
        revStart = -.37
        baseSpeed=60.0           # range 0.1 to 100.0  lower for more speed
        motorTime=0.002          # time motor is on
        K =0.997                 # K + K2 must = 1.0
        K2 = 1.0 - K
        (gyro_scaled_x, gyro_scaled_y, gyro_scaled_z, accel_scaled_x,
                accel_scaled_y, accel_scaled_z) = read_all()
        last_x = get_x_rotation(accel_scaled_x, accel_scaled_y, accel_scaled_z)
        last_y = get_y_rotation(accel_scaled_x, accel_scaled_y, accel_scaled_z)

        gyro_offset_x = gyro_scaled_x
        gyro_offset_y = gyro_scaled_y

        gyro_total_x = (last_x) - gyro_offset_x
        gyro_total_y = (last_y) - gyro_offset_y

        while SELF.run:                # set to False when exit called
                baseTime=time.time()
                (gyro_scaled_x, gyro_scaled_y, gyro_scaled_z, accel_scaled_x,
                        accel_scaled_y, accel_scaled_z) = read_all()
```

```python
            timeDif=time.time() - baseTime

            gyro_scaled_x -= gyro_offset_x
            gyro_scaled_y -= gyro_offset_y

            gyro_x_delta = (gyro_scaled_x * timeDif)
            gyro_y_delta = (gyro_scaled_y * timeDif)

            gyro_total_x += gyro_x_delta
            gyro_total_y += gyro_y_delta

            xRotation = get_x_rotation(accel_scaled_x, accel_scaled_y,
                    accel_scaled_z)
            yRotation = get_y_rotation(accel_scaled_x, accel_scaled_y,
                    accel_scaled_z)
#Complementary Filter K + K2 must total 1.0
            last_x= (K * (last_x + gyro_x_delta)) + (K2 * xRotation)
            last_y= (K * (last_y + gyro_y_delta )) + (K2 * yRotation)
            temp = last_y + 3.9             # Adjustment factor to get close to zero.
            print('temp ',temp)       # With level platform want to
            # oscillate between - and +. This value will vary day to day


#       Calculate PID output value
            Error = set_point - temp
            P_value = P * Error
            Derivator = Error
            D_value = D * (Error - Derivator)
            Integrator = Integrator + Error

            if Integrator > Integrator_Max:
                    Integrator = Integrator_Max
            elif Integrator < Integrator_Min:
                    Integrator = Integrator_Min

            I_value = Integrator * I
            retPID = P_value + I_value + D_value

            if abs(retPID) > 7.8:       # adjust for your point of no return
                    actRunSpeed = 100       # past point of balance, set power off
            else:
```

```python
                    actRunSpeed = baseSpeed

        if (temp <= fwdStart and temp >= revStart):
            print("at center")
            p20.ChangeDutyCycle(100)              # set power off
            p16.ChangeDutyCycle(100)
            p21.ChangeDutyCycle(100)
            p12.ChangeDutyCycle(100)
            sleep(motorTime)
        elif temp < fwdStart:
            print('forward')
            try:
                    p20.ChangeDutyCycle(100)          # set power off
                    p16.ChangeDutyCycle(100)
                    p21.ChangeDutyCycle(actRunSpeed)
                    p12.ChangeDutyCycle(actRunSpeed)
                    sleep(motorTime)
            except:
                    print ("ERROR fwdBOTH on")

        elif temp > revStart:
            print('reverse')
            try:
                    p21.ChangeDutyCycle(100)          #set to 0 power
                    p12.ChangeDutyCycle(100)
                    p20.ChangeDutyCycle(actRunSpeed)
                    p16.ChangeDutyCycle(actRunSpeed)
                    sleep(motorTime)
            except:
                    print ("ERROR revBOTH")
        else:
            print("should not be here")

def threadStart():
    r6050Th=Thread(target=run6050loop, name='loop6050',args=())
    r6050Th.setDaemon(True)      #set to True so that thread stops on exit
    try:
            r6050Th.start()
    except:
            print(sys.exc_info())
```

```python
def startMotor():
    if SELF.motorSwitch.get() == "Motors ON":
        SELF.motorSwitch.set("Motors OFF")
        GPIO.output(18, 0)
    else:
        SELF.motorSwitch.set("Motors ON")
        GPIO.setup(18, GPIO.OUT)
        GPIO.output(18, 1)

def stopALL():
    SELF.run = False
    sleep(.2)                    #pause, allow time to stop
    GPIO.cleanup()
    sleep(.2)                    #pause, allow time for clean up
    root.destroy()               #close tkinter window, also stops thread

if __name__=="__main__":
    root = Tk()
    root.title("Balance Bot")
    root.geometry("255x100+1+10")#width, height, x location, y location
    Button(root, text='EXIT', command=stopALL).grid(column=0,row=0)
    SELF.motorSwitch=StringVar()
    SELF.motorSwitch.set('Motors OFF')
    Button(root, textvariable=SELF.motorSwitch,
           command=startMotor).grid(column=3,row=0)
    threadStart()#tkinter is main thread, so we can stop program
    mainloop()
```

In the electronic software version I have included several additional programs for working with the MPU-6050. One reads all the registers on the chip and saves their settings to a text file. Another is a work in process that uses a tkinter window and provides for changing most of the setting while the chip is displaying the various values. PID, timing, etc.

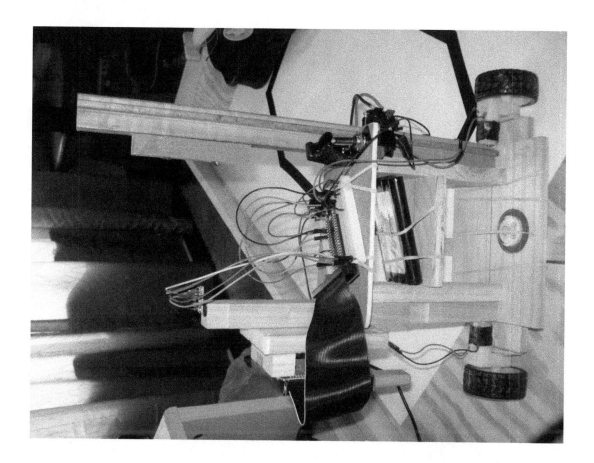

Thank You

While this book does contain the complete source code. The code in electronic or digital form is available for a limited time for an additional charge. On the web site http://www.rymax.biz/ click on the link to FastSpring. You will find the software listed under the same title as this book. Be sure to use the following discount code "HERB SAYS THANKS", this is a limited time special discount. The wiring diagrams are also included in color, which makes them much easier to read. Various pictures of the projects are included as well as some additional programs.